This book is a record of the wedding of

_____

and

_____

who were united in Holy Matrimony

at _____

_____

on _____ *19* _____

by _____

Reception followed at _____

_____

Your Complete Wedding Planner

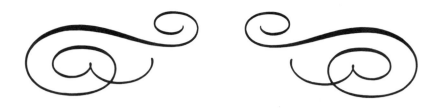

YOUR COMPLETE WEDDING PLANNER

For the Perfect Bride- and Groom-to-Be

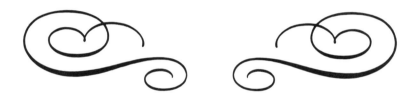

Marjabelle Young Stewart

David McKay Company, Inc.
New York

Library of Congress Cataloging in Publication Data

Stewart, Marjabelle Young.
    Your complete wedding planner for the perfect bride-
and groom-to-be.

    1. Wedding etiquette.   I. Title.
BJ2051.S73   395'.22   77–7304
ISBN 0–679–50813–9 gift ed.

Designed by Helen Roberts
Illustrations by Marika
Cover design by Alexander

10 9 8 7 6
Manufactured in the United States of America

To my precious daughter, Jacqueline Bryant Young; my dear son,
William Cullen Bryant Stewart; "Gram" Hazel Young Penry; my
mother-in-law, Elizabeth Stewart; and to the memory of my
beautiful mother, Marie Flint Bryant Hrasky, inventor, song writer,
wise counselor, and kind friend.

Acknowledgments

Over a period of five years—during the writing of this book—many friends have assisted me. Marrita DeRoo was of inestimable help in reading and editing the first draft and making suggestions for its improvement and getting me on the way. Special thanks to my friends Mrs. Claudia Buchanan for her help on flowers for the wedding; and Norma Blewett, journalist, for information on current wedding trends. Thanks also to Marion Faux, who helped write the book; Barbara Anderson, who edited it; and to Dominick Abel, my agent, who encouraged me to finish the book. Thanks also to my secretaries for the typing of thousands of words: Barbara Borkgren, Kathy Erickson, Mary Lou Ellis, Diane DeWitt, and Karen Knight.

What therefore God hath joined together,
let not man put asunder.
—Matthew 19:6

To have and to hold from this day forward,
for better, for worse, for richer, for
poorer, in sickness, and in health, to love
and to cherish, till death do us part.
—The Book of Common Prayer

Contents

Introduction

A wedding is an official and ceremonial commitment, a celebration of love shared between two people; it is a major production of theatrical proportions. A wedding requires thought, planning, and a great deal of loving care.

This book offers the guidelines and the help you need to plan every phase of the wedding and the events that surround it—engagement parties, showers, rehearsal dinner, reception, and even the honeymoon. There are suggestions for adding the personal touches that make a wedding more intimate, and advice about some of the practicalities of arranging your life so that it can be shared with another person. Included at the back of the book is a bride's organizer, a special section designed to help you plan and execute all the details that will make your wedding day nothing less than a dream come true.

Please notice that nowhere in this introduction—or even in the book—is there mention of the "rules" of etiquette. This is because the rigidity that so many young people have come to associate with etiquette has largely fallen away. Good manners have always meant kindliness and graciousness toward others, but they used to be backed with a list of rules that showed people how to behave. Now good manners, and particularly the "etiquette" of planning your wedding, are completely based on your feelings and attitudes. A modern bride has any kind of wedding she wants, but she also takes into consideration the feelings of others.

If you want to do something special for your wedding—such as having a song played that is not usually played at weddings—and it is in keeping with the dignity of the occasion, then go ahead. It is your wedding, and it should be planned in its minutest detail to satisfy you.

To your beautiful wedding,
Marjabelle Young Stewart

Your Complete Wedding Planner

1

The Beginning

When you were a young girl, you most likely envisioned your wedding day as something akin to a glowing, golden fairy tale. Every part of the event was glamorous and lovely. The princess married her prince and, of course, when the story ended, the charmed couple lived happily ever after.

Odd as it may seem, the only logical way to begin this book is with the destruction of the myth that a wedding is the happy ending in a fairy tale. A wedding marks the beginning of a marriage which will offer many joys—and sorrows. In marriage you share many of life's burdens with another person, but you also share the numerous responsibilities. Before you take the step of committing yourself to another person, be very sure that this is right for you.

Since a wedding is a beginning, you will want it to go as smoothly as possible. Too often, ill-planned weddings are marred by delays, bickering, and small details gone awry. A bride sometimes returns from her wedding trip faced with a mountain of thank-you notes to write and a mountain of gifts that she doesn't particularly like. When things go wrong, however, it usually is a result of the bride's not knowing her own mind. Before anyone can be expected to read your mind and help you plan the perfect wedding, you must learn to read it very carefully yourself.

Weddings have a way of escalating. Small, intimate gatherings can turn into large displays of opulence, and large, formal weddings can be reduced to tense, unhappy occasions. None of this need happen if you give careful thought to the life style of you and your groom and plan a wedding that is in keeping with it. If you and your fiancé are quiet, modest people who are more comfortable with casual living, chances are that you would prefer a small, relaxed wedding ceremony, rather than a formal affair. And if you want it, then you should have it! Your wedding belongs to you.

Your mother, aunts, and grandmothers may have definite ideas about the kind of wedding you should have. They should be handled as tactfully as possible, but this is *your* day, *your* wedding, and you should plan it to suit you.

This is also a time to give careful consideration to your family relationships. They may become strained at times during the wedding preparations, so if there has been a rift, now is the ideal time for detente. If you are old enough to marry, you are no longer a child, and that also means you can approach your parents as an adult.

Above all, try to retain a sense of humor about the wedding proceedings. Something is always bound to go wrong, but it won't seem nearly so disastrous if you are able to laugh and make the best of it.

Planning a wedding involves a lot of give and take. If you make some concessions to the feelings of others, they, in turn, will probably make some concessions to you. Once you are sure of what you want, be open to new ideas and suggestions, but don't let yourself be talked into something you really won't like.

Plan your wedding carefully and slowly. Think over the problems you confront and the best ways to solve them. Remember that weddings are a celebration of harmony—not disharmony.

Your Engagement

BREAKING THE NEWS

The first people to know of your wonderful decision should be your respective parents. Since many couples today live in cities or towns far from their parents, your parents may not have met your fiancé before you make the big announcement. If so, try to plan a trip home to introduce him and to break the news.

If his parents live in the same town as yours, it is customary for them to call on your parents. Don't stand on ceremony, however. If his mother does not call or write your mother, there is no reason why your mother cannot initiate the contact.

If you do bring your fiancé home with you, leave him alone with your father for a few minutes. You and your mother can go shopping or run a quick errand. Gone are the days when your fiancé will ask for your hand in marriage, but your father may welcome an opportunity to talk privately with the man you will marry.

Close relatives should be informed by note or phone, as should friends. Reading an announcement in the newspaper is not the way for your most intimate friends and relatives to learn the happy news. Once the word is out, you can wear your engagement ring.

THE RINGS

The engagement ring is a gift from your fiancé. Many women prefer not to have an engagement ring, but if you want one, and your fiancé can afford it, by all means you should have one. To avoid embarrassment over prices, your fiancé can go to the jeweler alone first and have a selection he can afford put aside for you to choose from when you return together. Your fiancé might also check into payment policies at this time since many jewelers now require a co-signer if the groom cannot pay cash for the ring.

The ring need not be the traditional diamond; any stone is appropriate as long as it is one you like and will cherish for many years to come. Also, when you select an engagement ring, keep in mind the kind of wedding ring you will want, since they are both worn together.

Your fiancé may offer you an heirloom engagement ring or wedding band. Many of these are beautiful old rings, but if the one you are offered runs counter to your taste, you may decline it. Say that you have always wanted to wear a ring you have chosen or something equally tactful.

Your groom's wedding band is a gift from you. It need not match yours but should be something that he has chosen.

Wedding rings are still frequently engraved. Your jeweler will be able to assist you with this.

AN ENGAGEMENT PARTY

A party is a lovely way to announce an engagement. Usually close friends and relatives will be aware that an announcement is in the offing, and when they receive an invitation, they will not be too surprised. Your parents or other close relatives usually give the engagement party. It may be announced as a party "honoring our daughter and her fiancé, Aaron," or your parents may simply invite everyone to a party. Midway through the party, by way of breaking the news, your father can propose a toast to you and your fiancé. The groom's family and yours and close friends of you and your parents should be invited to the engagement party, which can be as simple or as elaborate as your parents wish.

THE FORMAL ANNOUNCEMENT

Formal announcement of an engagement is usually made through a newspaper where you and your fiancé live and in both sets of parents' hometown newspapers. City newspapers today often don't give much space to these announcements. In fact, newspapers in many large cities will announce engagements and weddings only as a paid advertisement, costing $250 to $500, depending on the size of the announcement. A call to a society page editor will let you know whether or not you should send an announcement. Your parents issue the announcements in their names.

There are a few guidelines to follow in preparing a newspaper announcement. First, if you send a picture of yourself with the announcement, it should be a good 8 x 10-inch glossy print. Second, type the announcement, do not write it. Each newspaper should be given fresh copy; carbons are not flattering to the society editor who receives them. If you know the name of the society editor, by all means direct the press release to her personally. At the top of the announcement, put a release date. The newspaper is bound not to print the notice of your engagement before this date. All newspapers should be given the same release date.

Write the announcement as nearly as possible in the style of the newspaper to which it is submitted. This usually means that the most important information is given first and the less important details follow. Use your and your fiancé's full names; nicknames are not appropriate here. Be sure to give your fiancé's name and address and his parents' names and address.

In addition to the news of your engagement, some newspapers are interested in miscellaneous information about you such as the following:

Your and your fiancé's membership in clubs, fraternities, and sororities
Your and your fiancé's business affiliations
Your grandparent's names if they are distinguished socially or prominent in some other way
A distinguished ancestor
Military service of you or your fiancé
Your and your fiancé's fathers' business affiliations
Mention of your coming out, if you made a debut

(5)

An announcement should also include the date of the wedding, even if it is as tentative as "A summer wedding is planned."

If you are a minor, your mother's signature may be required on the announcement.

The following form shows the kind of release you can type yourself:

THE KEWANEE STAR-COURIER

Mr. and Mrs. Donald Park of 522 S. Tremont Street announce the engagement of their daughter, Miss Julia Lea Park, to Mr. Aaron Thomas Jones, son of Mr. and Mrs. Douglas Richard Jones of 333 McClure Street.

Miss Park is a graduate of the University of Chicago. Mr. Jones, a graduate of St. John's Military Academy, is a third-year law student at Harvard University.

If you prefer, you can fill out a copy of the engagement form that follows:

ENGAGEMENT FORM

Please fill out and return to Society Editor.

Full name of bride-elect ——————————— Phone ————

Residence of bride-elect ————————————————

Parents ————————————————————————

Parents' residence ——————————————————

College and prep schools ———————————————

Social affiliations —————————————————

Family connections —————————————————

Full name of bridegroom-elect ——————— Phone ————

Residence of bridegroom-elect ————————————

Parents ————————————————————————

Parents' residence ——————————————————

College and schools —————————————————

Social affiliations —————————————————

Family connections —————————————————

Date of wedding ——————————————————

How engagement is announced ——————————

Release date ————————————————————

Signature of bride-elect or one of her parents ——————

(Use reverse side for additional information.)

There is a special place in the bride's organizer to keep a copy of your engagement announcement.

Wedding Traditions

Planning a wedding is a major task, even though it's a particularly joyous one. Before you are caught up in the activity that inevitably surrounds most weddings, you might want to consider and perhaps select some of the traditions you want to follow at your wedding.

Few moments in one's life are as fraught with tradition as one's wedding day. Traditions add personal meaning to your wedding and also tie it together symbolically with all other weddings. Some traditions may have been handed down in your family, or you may have observed a custom that particularly appealed to you at another wedding. Or you can choose from among the many traditions described here.

The saying "Happy is the bride the sun shines on" is attributed to the belief held by ancient peoples in the fertilizing power of the sun. In some ancient cultures, the bride was required to rise early on her wedding day and "look into the face of the sun." Sometimes the betrothed greeted the sun together, and if the day happened to be a rainy one, the wedding was postponed in favor of a more auspicious time. Today, one naturally hopes a bride will have a sunny wedding day, but weddings are no longer postponed, and there is no record of a rainy day interfering with future happiness.

Most wedding customs symbolize the union of two persons. They are intended to reinforce the notion of fertility, constancy, and happiness.

The first wedding tradition you will probably follow is the selection of rings. The use of rings dates back to the days when a price was paid for a bride, and the earliest ones were made of braided grass. Diamond engagement rings first appeared in medieval Italy. An engagement ring, whether of diamond, that most durable of gems, or some other stone, symbolized partial payment for the bride and the groom's good intentions toward her.

Unending love has been symbolized by the unbroken circular wedding band since the days of the ancient Egyptians. Early Romans wore iron rings to symbolize the permanent relationship between a husband and wife, but affluent cultures have traditionally leaned toward a gold band.

Because ancient peoples believed that the vein in the third finger of the left hand led directly to the heart, the ring has traditionally been placed on that finger.

The English Book of Prayer in 1549 specified the left hand as appropriate for men and women, and since that time, English-speaking people have worn their rings on their left hands. In many Western European countries, however, the wedding ring is worn on the right hand. Greek women wear their rings on the left hand until they are married and then transfer them to the other hand.

The wearing of the wedding veil is an ancient custom, although its origins are vague. It undoubtedly originated as an expression of sexual modesty. Many ancient peoples believed that the bride should be completely hidden from the prospective husband's gaze until after the marriage ceremony, and in some countries, this practice is still followed. The custom of wearing a bridal veil is old and cherished and contributes much to the romantic aura of a wedding. It probably became a permanently fashionable custom in the United States when Nelly Custis wore a long veil to her wedding to Major Lawrence Lewis, President George Washington's aide. She chose the veil because her fiancé had made appreciative comments about her appearance after glimpsing her through a lace curtain at an open window.

Along with the veil, most brides choose a white wedding dress, which tradition holds is a symbol of purity of mind and body and a sign of celebration.

Probably the most familiar of wedding customs is contained in this poem describing what a bride should wear:

> Something old,
> Something new,

Something borrowed,
Something blue—
And a lucky sixpence in your shoe!

Rare is the bride who ignores this old rhyme, which holds the promise of a lifetime of joy and happiness. An heirloom handkerchief, veil, or prayer book is often the "something old," and many brides wear pearls or another simple piece of jewelry that was worn by a mother or grandmother on her wedding day. By tradition, the "something new" is usually the wedding dress, some of its accessories, or the bridal bouquet. "Something borrowed" is frequently a handkerchief, gloves, or some accessory lent to the bride by one of her attendants or another close friend. "Something blue" is usually a blue garter, but it can also be a delicate blue monogram on the bride's slip, a small bow of blue ribbon attached to the inside of her gown, or another small accessory. A silver dime tucked into the bride's shoe serves as the "sixpence" that ensures good fortune. Frequently the dime is saved to be passed on to a daughter, godchild, or niece.

Orange blossoms are the traditional wedding day flower. The belief that orange blossoms bring extra assurance of happiness stems from the Roman myth that the goddess Juno gave Jupiter a "golden apple" on their wedding day. The English poets Spenser and Milton have interpreted the "golden apple" as an orange.

In fourteenth-century France, one was considered lucky to win the bride's garter. Everyone rushed for it at the end of the ceremony. So serious was this tradition that people were often hurt in the scuffle, and the wise bride soon learned to leave one garter dangling so it could be easily reached, and eventually the bride began to throw the garter. Tossing the garter soon led to another custom, that of "stocking throwing," until brides began to rebel against a custom they considered undignified and embarrassing. Instead, they threw their bouquets, a custom that has persisted. Tradition holds that the person who catches the bouquet will be the next bride, so if you have someone special in mind (a sister or your maid of honor) you had better face the group and take careful aim. An impartial bride tosses the bouquet over her shoulder and leaves its recipient to fate.

When a woman was considered property and a price was paid for her, it was necessary for her father or guardian to give her—quite literally—to the groom. Today, the father walks his daughter to the altar and gives her in marriage as a sign of his approval of the union.

Several traditions surround the prenuptial festivities. The first bridal shower is believed to have taken place in Holland when a father disapproved of his daughter's choice of a poor miller as a life partner. When the father forbade the marriage, her friends "showered" her with gifts so she would have the traditional dowry she needed to set up housekeeping.

At either a bridesmaids' party given by the bride or at a shower, a pink cake is traditionally served, with a ring, thimble, or coin baked into it. Legend holds that woman whose piece of cake contains the trinket will be the next bride.

The bachelor party is a prevailing custom in many places today. Intended as a last fling, it, like the bridesmaids' party, also provides an opportunity for the groom to thank his attendants and to give them their gifts. A toast is proposed to the bride, and traditionally the glasses used for this toast are broken so they can never again be used for a less worthy purpose. If your fiancé plans to follow this custom, he should buy some inexpensive glasses for the purpose. Because of the amount of drinking that often takes place at the bachelor party, more and more grooms-to-be are holding this party two or three nights before their wedding day.

The trousseau, derived from the French word *trousse*, which means "bundle," originally was a bundle of clothes and housekeeping articles that the bride was expected to bring to her new home. Trousseaus expanded into dowries, which were often large enough to enhance the value of an unmarried daughter to her suitors. At one point, a trousseau was all the clothes a bride would need for one year, plus a generous amount of household linens—the finest the bride could afford. Today, a bride's trousseau usually consists of a few articles of new clothing, usually picked for her honeymoon or her social needs in her new home.

The origin of the tiered wedding cake is particularly charming. In medieval England, a bride and groom kissed over a small pile of cakes. An enterprising baker soon massed these cakes together and frosted them, thus giving birth to the modern tiered wedding cake.

In ancient times, rice and other grains were symbols of fertility. The Romans broke a thin loaf of wheat bread over the bride's head, and the crumbs were eagerly sought after by the guests as good-luck tokens. Throwing rice—a custom that has given way to throwing confetti or rose petals—was the guests' way of wishing the couple a productive life with many children.

Along with rice, there was a time when old shoes were also thrown at a bride. The shoe was a symbol of possession and authority. When a woman married, her father gave one of her old shoes to the groom to signify that authority over her was now transferred to him.

The custom of throwing rice and shoes after the couple has now lost its original significance, and the throwing of rice and tying of shoes to the back of the couple's car remain only as symbols of good luck.

In ancient Rome, the doorstep or threshold was the domain of Vesta, goddess of the hearth, who is associated with virgins. One can well imagine what a bad omen it was if a bride stumbled while entering her new house, so it became traditional for the groom to carry her across the threshold. It is a pleasant custom that is followed even today, although the superstition associated with it has long been forgotten.

There are some lovely European customs that American brides sometimes follow. Throughout Europe, couples ride to and from church in horse-drawn carriages decorated with flowers and ribbons. In England, bells peal as the bride enters the church to be married and again as she leaves it with her husband. In Belgium, a bride carries a small handkerchief embroidered with her name. The handkerchief is framed until the next family bride carries it and has her name embroidered on it.

In Bermuda, the new husband plants a small tree in the yard of their home. Its growth is a symbol of their growing love for each other.

Honeymoons originated in the days of the ancient Teutons, when couples were married under a full moon and drank honey wine for thirty days following the ceremony, or until the moon waned. From this comes the custom of today's wedding trip.

There is a special place in the bride's organizer to record the traditions you keep at your wedding.

4

Money—Who Pays for What

Perhaps because money is such a sensitive subject, it is more likely to be the cause of hurt feelings than any other part of a wedding. If the groom's parents do not know that they are expected to pay for the rehearsal dinner or the flowers for the mothers, they may harbor resentment over being asked to do so. On the other hand, if the bride's parents have set a limit to the number of guests for financial reasons and the groom's parents are not aware of this, they may inadvertently come up with a guest list that is beyond the bride's parents' means.

The best way to handle the costs of the wedding—specifically, who pays for what—is for the bride and her fiancé and possibly her parents, who share the greatest burden of expenses, to sit down and talk about what can be spent and who will spend it.

Finally, everyone should try to abide by the limits set. A groom's parents may indeed want to invite 300 friends even though the bride's parents have set the limit at 150 persons, but the party is being given by the bride's family, and the groom's family must abide by their limits. (If they are lucky, they will have a daughter for whom they can have the kind of wedding they want.)

The expenses generally attributed to the bride and her family include:

1. The engagement party
2. The engagement photograph

3. Gifts from the bride to the groom, including his wedding band, and those given to her parents and bridesmaids
4. Flowers carried by the bridesmaids and flowers decorating the church and the reception
5. Musicians at the church and the reception
6. Aisle carpet and ribbons at the church or reception; canopy or tent or any other similar accessories
7. Wedding photographs
8. Lodging for bridesmaids, if necessary
9. Transportation for the wedding party to and from the wedding reception
10. All expenses connected with the reception, including food, beverages, and room rental
11. Invitations, announcements, and personal stationery for the bride
12. The bride's wedding clothes and her trousseau

The bride may assume any or all of these expenses, according to her ability and desire to do so. The bride's family should make reservations for out-of-town guests but are not obliged to pay for their lodging. It is particularly nice to try to find free accommodations with local friends and relatives.

The groom or his family also have a set of expenses related to the wedding:

1. The bride's engagement and wedding rings and her wedding gift, if there is one
2. The marriage license
3. Gifts for the best man and ushers and the groom's parents, if he chooses to give them something
4. Matching ties and gloves for the ushers
5. The bride's bouquet and corsage, flowers for the mothers and grandmothers, and boutonnieres for the men in the wedding party
6. The clergyman's fee
7. The bachelor party
8. The rehearsal dinner
9. Overnight lodging for groomsmen if they come from out of town
10. The wedding trip (this expense is more and more frequently shared by the bride and groom, particularly if the bride works)

Choosing a Wedding You Can Afford

Barefoot brides and grooms are still being married on mountaintops here and there, but most couples are seeking out the old customs and planning traditional weddings, be they large or small.

A large, formal wedding is expensive, but a small informal wedding can also cost a lot of money, especially if you aren't aware of ways to keep the costs low.

There are several basic kinds of weddings to choose from:

1. Large, formal, and fancy. This is a church, synagogue or temple, or hotel wedding with all the trimmings, which generally includes most or all of the following: a large guest list, an elaborate dress, numerous attendants, engraved invitations and announcements, reception cards and at-home cards; a formal portrait and lots of photographs of the wedding taken by a professional photographer; a formal engagement portrait; lots of flowers at the wedding and the reception; limousines or another form of transportation for the entire wedding party; a large elaborate reception with musicians at which a meal is served.

2. Large, formal, and not quite so fancy. You could plan much the same wedding just described, but save a little by using recorded music at the reception and one musician at the wedding; an already existing portrait to announce your engagement; a professional wedding portrait, with candid shots being taken by an amateur photographer; a stand-up reception with punch and tea foods. The reception could be held in your home to further cut expenses.

3. Small, informal church wedding. You can have a small church or chapel wedding for a few relatives and friends, usually no more than fifty to seventy-five, and then have a small reception at home or in the church parlor or basement. Invitations could be handwritten or printed, and you could prepare all or part of the food yourself. Some churches now have their own wedding consultants or coordinators to help in planning.

4. Small, intimate wedding at home. Many charming weddings are intimate affairs with only a few close friends and the immediate family. Invitations are usually handwritten, and the reception could range from a simple tea to a fairly formal dinner.

COSTS OF WEDDINGS

Generally it is the reception that costs money, not the wedding itself. Before you decide on the type of wedding and reception you want, you should know a little bit about the costs that are involved. Depending upon the decisions you make, a small wedding could be just as expensive as a large one.

The average wedding-and-reception costs today run about $35 per guest, which includes a sit-down dinner. By shopping around, you can probably plan a reception for as little as $15 a head, and by doing everything yourself, you can cut costs even more.

It is difficult to pin down average costs because there are so many variables. A steak dinner costs more than a chicken dinner, for example, and simple bouquets cost far less than numerous elaborate arrangements. The least expensive reception is the stand-up afternoon tea. It has always been popular because of its low cost and simplicity.

Cost of Room and Refreshments

The first major cost will be the site of the reception. Most rooms rent for $50 to $200, but this fee is often dropped by a club or hotel if it caters the food and drinks. Some places offer a package price, usually around $2,500 or $3,000 for 200 guests. This fee includes everything—invitations, flowers, photos, and food and beverages. Some clubs rent by the hour, and you can usually count on the reception lasting about three hours.

Another arrangement is to rent a room and hire your own caterer, at a cost of about $11 to $15 per person, to handle the food and beverages.

In addition, there are caterers who specialize in ethnic wedding receptions, furnishing family-style dinners, open bar, and hall for about $8 to $10 per person. In such a case, you pay for the music separately.

Drinks are sold by the bottle and by the drink, with the price varying greatly. Check carefully to see what is the most economical way to wine your guests. Look into buying your own liquor from a dealer and hiring bartenders, if this is permitted.

Cost of Invitations

The typeface, paper, size, and number of extra card inserts determine the price of wedding invitations and announcements. Engraved invitations are more costly than printed ones. Invitations can be purchased for as little as $14.90 per 100, or as much as $100 to $150 per 100.

Cost of Flowers

Flowers can easily become a major wedding expense if they are not kept simple. Perishable or out-of-season flowers will have to be ordered specially, a factor that adds to their cost. An elaborate bridal bouquet that requires lots of wiring to hold its shape will be more expensive than a small, simple arrangement. The minimum price for a bridal bouquet is around $25. Attendants' bouquets average $15, and boutonnieres cost about $2.50 each for the groom and his best man, and about $1.25 each for the ushers. Altar baskets and table bouquets average $20. The church flowers can be carried to the reception, but they are more often donated to the church for the Sunday services.

Cost of Wedding Clothes

Three hundred dollars is the average cost for a bridal gown and veil. A bride who makes her dress and veil spends about one-third less.

Cost of Photographs

The money spent on photographs can vary from $90 for forty color photos and an album to $250 or more. A typical wedding package includes an 8 x 10 of the bride and groom, two 5 x 7s, and ninety-six 3½ x 5s, plus an album, for a cost of $120.50. A photographer with a "name" will be more expensive than one who is less well known.

Cost of Musicians

Most musicians must be paid union wages, which differ with the size and type of band but generally are no less than $100 for two to three musicians. An orchestra costs several thousand dollars, and an amateur soloist may cost as little as $35—or a gift from the bride and groom.

Cost of Wedding Cake

Purchased separately from a baker, the cake will run about $50. A home-baked cake or one made by a local amateur baker will cost less.

These are only rough estimates of average costs for the major items in a wedding reception. Remember that you must also buy bridesmaids'

ITEM	PRICE RANGE	
*Gown	$150–	$300
*Veil or headdress	35–	100
*Personal accessories	25–	75
*Gifts to bridesmaids	24–	120
*Bouquets for bridesmaids	96–	154
*Decorative flowers	100–	150
*Invitations	25–	75
*Organist	10–	50
Cars for bridal party	75–	100
Canopy for church entrance	100–	150
Sexton (rings the church bell, etc.)	25–	50
Pew ribbons	20–	35
Candles	25–	35
Aisle runner	25–	60
Formal photograph	50–	150
Tip to traffic officer	10–	25
TOTAL	$795–	1629

*Absolute essentials

(18)

gifts, arrange transportation for the wedding party on the day of the ceremony, and make a donation to the minister and church musicians. There will also be miscellaneous extra expenses. It always pays to shop around before you make final decisions, and to make this easier, in the bride's organizer you will find forms to keep a record of the cost estimates for various services. Also, remember that the purpose of the reception is to celebrate your wedding day with friends. A joyous occasion can be had just as well with homemade cake and simple punch as with an elaborate catered affair. A home or garden reception can be lovely and highly personal.

On the preceding page is an estimate of the total cost of a wedding and reception for 150 guests.

Tipping

In addition to the stated costs of a reception, you can expect to have to tip the people who serve you. The chart that follows shows the suggested amounts for tipping.

Person Tipped	Amount	Who Pays Tip
Caterer, hotel or club banquet manager, bridal consultant	1%–15%, only if special services are offered	Reception host adds any special payment to bill when he pays it
All servers, including waiters, waitresses, bartenders, and table captains	15% for servers plus 1%–2% for captains if their fee is not included in the total bill	Reception host adds gratuities to bill when he pays it
Powder and coat room attendants	50¢ per guest to each attendant, or a flat fee can be arranged with the hotel or club manager	Reception host adds flat fee to bill when he pays it; otherwise, attendants are tipped right after reception
Florist, photographer, baker, musicians, limousine driver	15% for drivers; 1%–15% for others only if special services are	Drivers should be tipped at the reception by host; other tips

Person Tipped	Amount	Who Pays Tip
	performed (delivery of flowers and cake is not usually considered a special service)	should be added to bill when paid
Civil ceremony officials such as judges, justices of the peace, and city clerks	A flat fee (usually $10 is the minimum) is paid, but check first to see if the official can accept money	Groom pays via his best man after the ceremony
Clergymen	Usually a donation based on your hourly income and dependent upon the time the clergyman has spent with you and on the size of the ceremony	Groom pays, either during the last meeting or through his best man, who pays before or after the ceremony
Ceremony assistants such as altar boys, and organists	($5–$25) The church often covers this fee, but check with the clergyman to see what is appropriate	These tips are paid directly after the service by the wedding host
Custodians and kitchen help if the reception is held in the church	Ask the church secretary—these fees are usually set	

A DO-IT-YOURSELF RECEPTION

As wedding costs have soared, more and more brides have chosen to arrange their weddings themselves. Often they write their own invitations, make their own and their attendants' outfits, bake the cake, arrange the flowers, and prepare the food. Music can be provided by tapes. What a bride does not own, she usually borrows for her reception—such things as silver serving pieces, candelabra, and serving tables. You can make your own tablecloths and decorate your home yourself. Such weddings are always charming, perhaps because they are so highly personal. They are also a wonderful way to save money. The costs for a do-it-yourself wedding for fifty are as follows:

ITEM	PRICE RANGE
Gown	$ 45– $50
Head covering	5– 10
Accessories	25– 50
Maid of honor's gift	10– 25
Bride's bouquet	0– 0
Maid of honor's bouquet	0– 0
Flowers for mantel and tables	0– 0
Invitations and stamps	5– 15
Champagne	55– 75
Cake	0– 0
Refreshments (ice cream, nuts, mints)	20– 40
Service for occasion	0– 0
Photographer	20– 20
TOTAL	$185–$285

Chapter 11 is devoted entirely to planning and executing your own reception.

6

Schedules and Appointment Sheets

Even the simplest wedding takes time to arrange—more time than most newly engaged men and women ever expected to have to spend on their weddings. One of the best ways to keep tract of everything and to make sure that everything is done on schedule is to refer frequently to the time charts in this chapter. Although three months may seem like a lot of lead time for planning a wedding, it is necessary if you want to be sure of obtaining services from the people who do them best. Also, many things related to a wedding must be special-ordered—the bride's wedding dress, the bridesmaids' dresses, the flowers, the invitations, the food —so time must be allowed to complete all the details.

Approach the scheduling of your wedding in an orderly way. Call in advance for appointments with the people with whom you must meet. That way they will be able to set aside some time to spend with you. They will appreciate your consideration of their time, and it will probably mean better service to you in the long run. On pages 151–52 of the bride's organizer, you'll find a place to keep track of all the names, addresses, and appointments related to your wedding and reception.

The lists that follow should help you organize the many details of your wedding.

AS SOON AS POSSIBLE

1. Meet with the clergyman to set a date; arrange for premarital instruction if necessary.
2. Draw up an overall wedding budget with your parents.
3. Decide on the formality, size, and location of your wedding and reception.
4. Decide on the number of guests, draw up your own guest list and request a guest list from the groom's family.

THREE TO FOUR MONTHS
BEFORE THE WEDDING

1. Reserve the place for the reception.
2. Reserve the caterer. Get lists of services and menu possibilities to look over before you make your final decision.
3. Book the musicians for the wedding and reception.
4. Ask the people you want to attend you if they will do so.
5. Order your invitations and announcements, also any other stationery you will need. Don't forget to order informals with your maiden name to use before the wedding and additional informals with your married name to use after the wedding.
6. Meet with the florist.
7. Meet with the photographer.
8. Meet with the baker.
9. Talk over honeymoon plans with your fiancé and make reservations as soon as you have decided where to go.
10. Shop for your wedding outfit and your attendants' outfits. Mothers should also be shopping for their dresses at this time.
11. If you plan to use contraceptives, see your doctor.

TWO MONTHS BEFORE THE WEDDING

1. Firm up any last-minute arrangements for the menu, flowers, and wedding cake for the reception.
2. Begin to address invitations; they should be mailed no later than three weeks before the day of the wedding.
3. Register your preferences for gifts.
4. Select your wedding bands and order any engraving you want on them. Select your attendants' gifts.
5. Get your trousseau together. Buy any new clothes you will need and be sure clothes you already own are in perfect shape. Plan and, if necessary, buy your going-away outfit.
6. Schedule and have the final fitting on your wedding dress and the attendants' dresses, if possible.
7. Have your wedding portrait taken.
8. Ask people to serve on the hospitality committee.
9. Double-check all arrangements. Call the caterer, baker, photographer, and florist to remind them and to confirm any last-minute changes. Make final selections for the music to be played at the wedding and reception and inform the musicians.
10. Put your financial affairs in order. Transfer or add your name to insurance policies, arrange bank and checking accounts, notify Social Security Administration, charge accounts, driver's license bureau, voter registration board, post office, clubs, etc., of your new name.
11. Arrange lodging for out-of-town guests. Book and pay for any rooms for attendants.
12. Arrange transportation for out-of-town guests to and from airports, train stations, etc. (See pages 154–55 of bride's organizer.) Plan, too, for their entertainment.
13. Arrange transportation for all members of the wedding party to and from the ceremony and reception. (See page 153 of bride's organizer.)
14. Send maps showing the way from the church to the reception to out-of-town guests, but don't enclose these with the invitations.

ONE MONTH BEFORE THE WEDDING

1. Order any special things you will need—candles, extra greenery, guest book, silver serving pieces, tables for reception, ashtrays. Check all details just as you would for any other party. Plan tablecloths for guests' tables and bride's table if this will not be taken care of by the caterer.
2. Pick up the marriage license; have any tests required by the state and a medical examination if you need one.
3. Make bags of rose petals or rice for tossing as you leave the reception.
4. Pick up any tickets or reservations needed for your honeymoon.
5. Plan the details of the rehearsal dinner and invite people who will attend.
6. Plan the open house at your parents' home after the wedding. Usually this party is held for close friends and relatives immediately after the formal reception, but it may also be held the next day, particularly if a large number of out-of-town guests will be staying over.
7. Mail wedding invitations to guests.
8. Send the wedding announcement with your portrait to the newspapers at least three weeks before the wedding. (See page 156 of the bride's organizer.)
9. Be sure your wedding outfit is in order—shoes dyed, jewelry selected, any special accessories ordered.
10. Make appointment for haircut and styling the morning of your wedding, or one or two days before.
11. Arrange for a policeman to direct traffic at the church and reception sites.

ONE TO TWO WEEKS
BEFORE THE WEDDING

1. Wrap gifts for attendants.
2. Begin packing for your honeymoon.

3. Give the reception manager or caterer a final estimate of the number of guests expected.
4. Make sure wedding announcements (if used) are ready for your parents to mail after the wedding.
5. Make arrangements for wedding gifts, furniture, and personal belongings to be moved to your new home.
6. Make a final check with everyone concerned with the wedding to see that everything is in order.

Aside from the myriad of details to be attended to, you will be attending parties in your honor and having the time of your life being the center of attention. Enjoy yourselves!

7

The Attendants and the Ceremony

As soon as you have selected the date and time for the wedding, you and your fiancé should decide how many attendants you want and need, and you should ask them to participate. Once your attendants have accepted, it is time to begin planning the ceremony itself. More and more couples are taking an active interest in the ceremony, rewriting old vows or writing new ones, departing from the traditional wedding music, and adding special touches that make it very much their special day. Plan some long, leisurely dinners together to talk over the meaning of your ceremony and exactly how you want it to be.

THE TIME OF DAY

There are few restrictions today regarding the time of day when you can be married or even the day. Your clergyman or someone in his office will be happy to give any information about days that are not acceptable for weddings. For example, large formal weddings are generally not held on Christmas Day or Easter or during Lent. Jewish weddings are not held on the Sabbath (Saturday) or on certain holy days or festival days.

There used to be fashionable times of day for weddings. Fortunately, most of these rules have been forgotten, and today's bride can be married at any time of day she chooses.

A wedding held about noon is followed by a breakfast, which may be either a formal seated affair or a buffet. A late afternoon wedding at two, three, or four o'clock is followed by a reception where light refreshments—cocktail and tea tidbits—are served. A wedding at or around six o'clock is followed by a dinner and dance. The dinner is usually a seated event, but a buffet may be served as long as the food is substantial enough.

After eight o'clock, a dance and late-night supper are called for. Lavish cocktail food or a supper should be served to guests.

CHOOSING THE ATTENDANTS

There are no set rules about the number of attendants; it usually depends upon the degree of formality and the size of your wedding. Ushers are selected with an eye toward seating guests; one usher is required for every fifty guests. The number of ushers need not match the number of bridesmaids unless you plan to have them walk together in the recessional.

Attendants may be single or married, and they are usually about the same age as the bride and groom. They are always close friends or relatives, because considerable expense is involved in being an attendant and one may not refuse without a very good reason, such as absence from the country, another family commitment, or recent death in the family. Call or write your attendants, or ask them in person. Be sure to specify the date and time of the wedding and the degree of formality. If an attendant cannot afford to accept (attendants generally pay for their outfits and their transportation to and from the wedding), he or she may tell you this directly, if the relationship is comfortable enough to do so, or may claim a prior and important family function of his or her own. An invitation to participate in a friend's wedding should not be accepted —or declined—lightly. If you must decline, do so with sincerest and most tactful regrets. Make the bride or groom feel that you truly would like to be part of such an important, meaningful day if it were at all possible.

Once attendants have been invited to participate, they are treated as honored guests. They—and their husbands and wives—receive invitations to the wedding, rehearsal dinner, and any other festivities that surround the wedding. The exception is showers. If they are numerous, a thoughtful bride will invite her attendants to only one or two showers and will indicate to them that either no gift or only a very small gift is expected.

In the bride's organizer you'll find a place for the names, addresses, and phone numbers of all your attendants.

THE BRIDE'S ATTENDANTS

The bride is attended by a maid or matron of honor, who is her main attendant, one or more bridesmaids or junior bridesmaids, and a flower girl (or girls), if she chooses.

Maid of Honor

The maid of honor is usually the bride's sister, a cousin, or her closest friend. If the person is married, she is called the matron of honor. The maid of honor is the bride's personal attendant during the ceremony. She moves the bride's veil if needed, holds her bouquet during the ceremony, and keeps the groom's ring, if there is one. She may be distinguished from the bridesmaids by a slight variation in the style or color of her dress or by slightly different flowers. Or her outfit and flowers may be the same as those of the bridesmaids.

Bridesmaids and Junior Bridesmaids

Bridesmaids are generally about the same age as the bride and they are her close friends, although she frequently invites a cousin to whom she is close and a relative, usually a sister, of the groom.

A junior bridesmaid is usually a sister or cousin under the age of sixteen and as young as ten or eleven. Her duties are exactly the same as the other bridesmaids—to be a lovely and joyous addition to the wedding party and to mingle with the guests during the reception.

Bridesmaids pay their own expenses to and from the wedding; lodging is usually arranged for and paid by the bride's family. Bridesmaids purchase all of their outfits, except for the flowers, which are provided by the bride's parents. It is perfectly acceptable for the bride's parents to pay for the expenses for any or all of the bridesmaids, but it is seldom done.

The Flower Girl

One or more flower girls are a particularly touching gesture. Although a flower girl can be any little girl from the age of four to eight, maturity and poise should be a major factor determining your choice. A child who is shy or frightened may balk at the moment when she has to walk down the aisle or may cause some disturbance during the ceremony. The flower girl, usually a sister, cousin, or niece of the bride or groom, carries a small bouquet or scatters rose petals as she goes down the aisle. Her dress is anything appropriate for a young child that is in keeping with the color and style of the wedding.

THE GROOM'S ATTENDANTS

The groom selects a best man, ushers, and possibly a small boy as ring bearer.

The Best Man

Thought should be given to the selection of the best man, as he will more or less be the mastermind on the day of the wedding. The best man, usually the groom's brother or close friend, and only rarely his father, calls for the groom on the day of the wedding, helps him dress, and accompanies him to the wedding. He makes sure the ushers are properly dressed and versed on their duties; he carries the wedding ring in a convenient place so he can produce it with a minimum of fumbling at the proper moment. He pays the minister, and he may carry such items as the bride and groom's car keys, their travel tickets, and their marriage license. During the reception, he generally offers a toast to the bride and groom; often, he is expected to initiate the toasts.

The Ushers

Ushers, selected by the groom from among his close friends and relatives or from the bride's relatives, are part of the bridal procession. They escort guests as they arrive and exit, offering their arms to women regardless of whether or not they are escorted by another man.

    The ushers, like the bridesmaids, should show concern for the comfort of the guests. Unattended women should be asked to dance by the ushers.

Groomsmen provide their own clothing, either purchased or rented, although matching ties and gloves are generally provided by the groom as a gift to his attendants. Out-of-town attendants are expected to provide their own transportation, although the father of the groom may offer to pay for outfits and transportation for one or all of the groomsmen. Flowers for the groomsmen are provided by the groom's parents. Arrangements for lodging are usually made and paid for by the groom; attendants can stay with close friends or relatives or in a hotel.

A ring bearer, who can be any boy from about four to seven years old who has the social poise to handle the occasion, walks in the processional and carries the ring, securely sewn on a small white pillow. His outfit is similar to or the same as those of the groomsmen, or he may wear short pants or something of his own that is in keeping with the formality of the wedding.

Some special attentions are necessary for the ring bearer and flower girl. They and their parents are invited to the rehearsal dinner, and special arrangements for their transportation should be made. As a remembrance, each child should be given a small gift and a photo taken with the bride and groom.

THE UNOFFICIAL ATTENDANT

Contributing to the overall success of the wedding and reception should be some kind of supervisor-general, usually an aunt, older sister, godmother, or good and trustworthy friend. Such a person can graciously handle the details of the receiving line, signal the time to cut the cake, make the toasts, start the music for the first dance, remind others of the order of dances, and see that pictures are taken of everyone the bride and groom want pictures of. The person who graciously accepts your invitation to oversee the wedding should make things run smoothly and should be given complete charge, but she should take care not to upstage the mother of the bride, who is the official hostess. This person should be given a gift and photo taken of her with the bride and groom.

MUSIC DURING THE CEREMONY

Since the music played before and during the processional and recessional can set the entire tone of the wedding ceremony, you will want to take care to select music you truly enjoy, music that is in keeping with the religious significance of the wedding. When you meet with the clergyman, ask his views on music that he considers suitable. Then plan to meet with the musicians, usually an organist, and occasionally one or more instrumentalists and a soloist. Discuss the music you want played; listen to them play or sing part or all of it, and decide what you would like played and in what order. Generally about fifteen to thirty minutes of music are planned for the time when guests are arriving; a march is needed for the processional and the recessional. Select music that you and your groom appreciate; do not take the advice of others if it is contrary to what you want.

If the musical program is complicated, a full rehearsal may be in order. If you have hired professionals, the church's regular musicians, or students from a nearby musical school, some payment is expected. If the musicians are friends, a gift is in order.

Favorite selections for music prior to the ceremony include *Arioso* by Bach, Preludes on Antiphone by Dupré, Aria in F Major by Handel, or any other music you particularly like. A favorite song of the betrothed couple may be played or sung. If a vocalist is used, he or she sings about ten to fifteen minutes before the ceremony and again just before the mother of the bride is seated.

Processional music should be joyous yet dignified. The entrance music as the bride begins her walk down the aisle is traditionally the bridal chorus from Wagner's *Lohengrin*. Other popular processionals include the Air from the Water Music Suite by Handel, Trumpet Voluntary in D by Purcell, and Rigaudon by Campra. The music is played softly as the attendants come down the aisle, and changes in content or volume to announce the bride. Music is sometimes played softly during the vows, but you should check with the clergyman before making plans for this.

Recessional music is quicker in tempo and livelier than the processional. Popular recessionals are the Wedding March from *Midsummer Night's Dream* by Mendelssohn, Ode to Joy from Symphony no. 9 by Beethoven, and Trumpet Voluntary in D by Purcell. In recent years, the

Mendelssohn wedding march has been frowned upon by purists who feel that it is not in keeping with the religious nature of the service. Such opinions do not seem to have hindered its popularity, and if you want it and your clergyman agrees, have it played. It is your wedding.

Other secular pieces of music that are increasingly played at weddings today, often to the accompaniment of a guitar, include the themes from *Love Story* and *Romeo and Juliet*, "Annie's Song" by John Denver, "My Sweet Lady," "Sunrise Sunset," "We've Only Just Begun," or "More." Cat Stevens's "Morning Has Broken" and Paul Stookey's "Wedding Song" are other popular choices.

There is such a wide variety of possible music that you may find yourself confused. If so, a trip to the library or a local music store where you can listen to recordings is in order. Most libraries have collections of fine music that can be checked out. A call to a high school or college music teacher or the church organist can also unearth some helpful information.

You should not feel embarrassed at not knowing what music is appropriate, nor should you be afraid to take your doubts to people whose business is to know. They will be glad to help you.

Generally a month should be allowed between the final selection of the music and the ceremony. In the bride's organizer, you'll find a place to write out a list of the music chosen and the order in which you would like it played. Give one copy to the musicians and keep one for yourself.

You may want to spend a little time practicing walking to the music you have chosen. If possible, obtain a record of the music and play it frequently to become accustomed to it. Wedding music is highly emotional, and many brides have cried their way to the altar because of the sudden effect the music has had on them. It might also be a good idea to tell your father you need to practice walking on his arm to the music and give him a chance to get used to it, too. Elaborate wedding walks are unpopular today, but a lovely bride will want to have an aura of confidence about her ability to float down the aisle to the music she has chosen.

Music is as important to the reception as to the wedding, and reception music is discussed in chapter 9.

PLANNING THE VOWS

Your religion and your clergyman will most probably set forth the nature and type of vows you exchange, but more couples today are giving serious thought to their vows, and many are even writing their own. Before you embark on such a major venture, consult with your clergyman to see if this is permissible. At a minimum, you may want to arrange a special meeting with the clergyman to discuss your vows and any extra passages that you want to include. Most clergymen are delighted to talk with couples who give such serious consideration to their vows.

Invitations and Announcements

SELECTING THE GUESTS

Once you have chosen the date, time, and place of your wedding, it is time to begin preparing a guest list. If your wedding is to be large enough for you to invite everyone you want to, lucky you. If not, you will have to do a little tactful sorting out. First on your list will probably be relatives, followed by close family friends, the people who have watched you grow up and participated in your life at other meaningful stages. You will also want to include your dear friends—and your mother will want to include her dear friends, and the groom's mother will have a similar list. The clergyman and his wife are invited to the wedding and reception, as are the husbands and wives of married attendants. The parents of the flower girl and ring bearer are invited to the wedding and reception. Parents of unmarried attendants are invited to the wedding and reception, if they live nearby. Technically, the bride and groom share the list equally—that is, each invites half the guests. In practice, the bride is more likely to take a larger share of the guest list, and there will probably be names added to the list jointly by you and your fiancé. If your fiancé's family lives far away, it is probably perfectly all right for you to take a larger share of the guest list. Otherwise, you will have to do whatever negotiating is required.

To be sure you haven't forgotten someone dear to you, make a last-minute check through your address book and your old Christmas card lists as well as those of your parents; go through alumni directories and club membership lists, too, to see if there is anyone you have missed.

Often there are some fuzzy areas on guest lists—people you aren't sure whether or not to invite. Usually these are people with whom you or your fiancé work, neighbors who are friends only by virtue of proximity, and out-of-town friends. If your guest list is small, you probably won't ask any of these people. Sometimes, when the guest list is limited, it is better not to ask anyone from a group—the people you work with, for example—than to ask only some of the people. On the other hand, if you have a co-worker to whom you feel especially close, by all means include him or her. Out-of-towners will probably be flattered to be asked to your wedding if they're close friends. On the other hand, since an invitation·makes most people feel that they must send a gift, you may not want to send announcements to out-of-town friends if you know they cannot possibly attend your wedding.

THE KIND OF INVITATION

Invitations are one of the more complicated aspects of a wedding, but by following a few simple procedures, this task can easily be sorted out.

If your wedding is very small—just the immediate families and a few friends—you may want to call or write personal notes to invite people. Either you or your mother as the official hostess can issue these informal invitations. Even if you write them, they should be issued in your mother's name.

Written invitations are usually engraved or thermographically printed. Invitations prepared in this way should be sent three to four weeks before the wedding, and it could take as long as eight weeks to engrave or print the invitations. Remember to request that envelopes be sent to you as soon as possible. That way you can have them addressed and ready to mail as soon as the invitations are printed. Don't forget, too, to order several extra invitations as keepsakes for you, your mother, and your groom's mother.

Another possibility for a wedding invitation is to handletter your own, if you have taken a course in calligraphy. Carefully prepare a sample copy and then shop around for a printer to reproduce it. (You could also have a professional calligrapher write your invitation for a cost of about $35 to $50.) Calligraphers are listed in the phone book, as are printers and engravers.

The printer or engraver will show you samples of types and papers from which you may choose. Wedding invitations are often set in a rather traditional script typeface, although many brides today are choosing a more modern typeface. As long as the type and paper are conservative and in keeping with the formality of your wedding, choose whatever you like. Below are several typefaces that are excellent for invitations.

Mr. and Mrs. Michael Frank Natale

Mr. and Mrs. William H. Weissler

Mr. and Mrs. Richard G. Manning

Mr. and Mrs. Benjamin Getz

Mr. and Mrs. Michael Anthony Napolitano

Mr. and Mrs. Nathan L. Gruskoff

Mr. and Mrs. Vincent J. Vitolo

WORDING THE INVITATION

If both parents are living and still married to each other and this is your first marriage, your invitation is as follows:

Mr. and Mrs. Henry Robert James
request the honour of your presence
at the marriage of their daughter
Barbara Ann
to
Mr. Ronald John Borkgren
on Saturday, the third of June
at three o'clock
Visitation Church
Four hundred ten West Central Boulevard
Kewanee, Illinois

(37)

The church street address may or may not be included on the invitation. If it is, it should be spelled out. The year can be left off the invitation, but should be included on the announcement of the marriage. The word *honour* is always spelled with the *u*.

THE RECEPTION CARD

If the reception is held immediately after the wedding in the church, this information may be included on the wedding invitation. A joint wedding-reception invitation would read this way:

Mr. and Mrs. John Davison Young
request the honour of your presence
at the marriage of their daughter
Jacqueline
to
Mr. E. Russell Anderson
on Saturday, the seventeenth of September
at four o'clock
First Congregational Church
Silver Spring, Illinois
and afterward at breakfast
at Midland Country Club

R.S.V.P.
312 Quaint Acre's Drive
Silver Spring, Illinois 61443

More common is the practice of enclosing a reception card, which contains information about the celebration. The reception card, about half the size of the invitation, is identical in type, paper, and printing style to the invitation.

A card announcing a reception held in the bride's home would read:

Reception
immediately following the ceremony
522 South Tremont
Kewanee, Illinois 61443

R.S.V.P.

(38)

The card for a reception held in a club or hotel would read:

Reception
immediately following the ceremony
The Midland Country Club

R.S.V.P.
522 South Tremont Street
Kewanee, Illinois 61443

A separate reception card is used when only some of the guests at the wedding are invited to the reception.

If a meal is to be served at the reception, this should be noted on the invitation. If the reception is a luncheon or dinner, you can add the words "and luncheon" or "and dinner" after reception on the card.

If it is a breakfast, the following form might be used:

Mr. and Mrs. John Davison Young
request the pleasure of your company
at the wedding breakfast of their daughter
Jacqueline
and
Mr. E. Russell Anderson
on Saturday, the third of June
at one o'clock
Creve Coure Club
Peoria, Illinois
R.S.V.P.
312 Quaint Acre's Drive
Silver Spring, Illinois 61443

UNUSUAL INVITATIONS

Usually an invitation is issued jointly by the bride's parents. There are exceptions, and these make a difference in the wording of the invitations.

If one parent has died, the living parent issues the invitation. If the living parent has remarried, the invitation may be issued jointly, but the line reading "at the marriage of their daughter" would read "at the marriage of her (his) daughter." Usually if one parent died when the bride was very young and a stepparent has reared her, or if, for any

(39)

reason, their relationship is close, the invitation is issued in both the parent's and the stepparent's names.

If neither parent is alive, a wedding invitation is issued by grandparents, an aunt and uncle, older brother or sister, or even by the groom's family. Sometimes the bride and groom issue such an invitation themselves.

An invitation may be issued jointly by divorced parents if that is the bride's preference. If your mother has remarried, it would read:

Mrs. William Eugene Stewart
and
Mr. Jack Davison Young
request the honour of your presence
at the marriage of their daughter
Jacqueline

If your mother has not remarried, it should be issued as follows, using her maiden name and your father's name:

Mrs. Walsh Stewart
and
Mr. William Stewart
request the honour of your presence

If you have been divorced and your parents are sponsoring the wedding, the invitations should read:

Mr. and Mrs. Charles James Hughes
request the honour of your presence
at the marriage of their daughter
Jean Hughes Brown

If you are widowed and your parents are sponsoring the wedding, the invitations should read:

Mr. and Mrs. Charles James Hughes
request the honour of your presence
at the marriage of their daughter
Jean Louise Hughes

If you have been divorced and are sponsoring your own wedding, the invitations should read:

The honour of your presence
is requested at the marriage of
Mrs. Hughes Brown

(40)

If you are widowed and are sponsoring your own wedding, the invitations should read:

The honour of your presence
is requested at the marriage of
Mrs. David Michael Brown

The status of the groom—whether he has been widowed or divorced—has nothing to do with the invitations. His full name is always used.

DOUBLE WEDDING INVITATIONS

Sometimes two sisters or good friends are married in the same ceremony. Sisters usually issue joint invitations, and friends may or may not do this. If they do, the older woman's name usually appears first on the invitation. Sample invitations follow:

Mr. and Mrs. Charles James Hughes
request the honour of your presence
at the marriage of their daughters
Jean Louise
to
Mr. William Keith Summers
and
Joan Marie
to
Mr. Stanford Gerald Forrest

A joint invitation of friends would read:

Mr. and Mrs. Harry H. Blancher
and
Mr. and Mrs. Ronald Dewitt
request the honour of your presence
at the marriage of their daughters
Stacy Marie Blancher
to
Mr. Richard Harold Smith
and
Amy Ann Dewitt
to
Mr. Steven Michael Brown

A particularly nice custom has arisen of sending wedding invitations in the names of both sets of parents. Such an invitation would read:

Mr. and Mrs. Harry H. Blancher
and
Mr. and Mrs. Ronald Smith
request the honour of your presence
at the marriage of their children
Stacy Marie Blancher
to
Mr. Richard Harold Smith

The only drawback to this quite sensible custom is that frequently the parents who are paying for the wedding feel it is their prerogative to issue the invitations. Certainly it is up to them to suggest the idea of joint invitations.

On rare occasions, the groom's family issues the invitations to a wedding. This usually occurs when the bride is from overseas and has no family or when the bride has no close family to issue invitations for her. In such rare cases, it is acceptable for the bride to accept the offer of the groom's family to give her wedding. The invitation would read:

Mr. and Mrs. Roger Johnston
request the honour of your presence
at the marriage of
Miss Angela Dawn Erickson
to
their son
Bruce Eugene Johnston

MILITARY INVITATIONS

Armed Forces

When the groom is a commissioned officer in the United States armed forces, the invitations and announcements give his title. If the officer's rank is lieutenant colonel or above in the Army, commander or above in the Navy, Merchant Marine, or Coast Guard, or major or above in the Marine Corps, the title is used before his name:

Captain William Cullen Bryant Stewart
United States Army

Mention of the branch of service is optional.

If the groom holds a rank in the Army below those described, his name appears on a single line with his title set separately on the line below:

William Cullen Bryant Stewart
Second Lieutenant, United States Army

If the groom holds a rank below that of commander in the Navy, his rank also appears on a single line:

William Cullen Bryant Stewart
Lieutenant, junior grade, United States Navy

Members of Annapolis, West Point, or the U.S. Air Academy Graduating Class

If a graduate is married the day of or a few days after his commissioning, he may use his rank on the wedding invitation.

R.O.T.C. and N.R.O.T.C. Officers

A new reserve officer receiving a commission and awaiting the commencement of his obligated training tour cannot use his rank and branch designation on wedding invitations or have a military wedding in uniform. This regulation pertains to the period between graduation and the assignment to active duty, which may be several weeks or months. He may properly be identified, however, by rank and branch designation if, as a new reserve officer, he is in fact on active duty at the time of the wedding.

Retired Regular Army and Navy Officers

Retired high-ranking Army and Navy officers retain their titles in civilian life:

Commodore William Cullen Bryant Stewart
United States Navy, Retired

Or:

> Lt. General William Cullen Bryant Stewart
> United States Marine Corps, Retired

Retired or Inactive Reserve Officers

Unless they are colonels or above, their former titles may not be used.

Noncommissioned Officers and Enlisted Men

Noncommissioned officers and enlisted men use only their names with the branch of service immediately below, and "Mr." is omitted before the name:

> Dr. and Mrs. James B. Hopping
> request the honour of your presence
> at the marriage of their daughter
> Heidi Jo
> to
> William Cullen Bryant Stewart
> United States Marine Corps

The Bride in Military Service

The bride uses her military title in wedding invitations and announcements, as do men in service, with her identifying branch of service.

NO INVITATIONS

Although many urban newspapers no longer announce weddings and engagements, most small-town papers continue this tradition, and they inadvertently offer the betrothed couple a way to hold down expenses for their wedding. When a paper permits it, the couple can include the following statement in the engagement notice, by way of a wedding invitation:

> No invitations are being sent, but all friends and relatives of the couple are invited to attend the wedding and reception.

(44)

If the wedding is to be private, that fact should be announced in a newspaper story. To ensure privacy, sometimes the time and place of the wedding are withheld until they are printed in the wedding announcement.

When only a small reception is planned and the wedding has been announced through the papers, it is more tactful not to mention the reception at all. Only those who are invited to the reception need know the details of it.

If you decide to announce your wedding and invite guests in this manner, it is a good idea also to send notes to people you especially want to attend. If written notes are sent, they are written on heavy white paper in black or dark blue ink. They should be issued by the mother of the bride or in her behalf and could read as follows:

Dear Sue,

Rusty and Jackie are being married very quietly here at the house, 522 South Tremont Street, on Saturday, September 19, at 2 P.M. Bill and I so hope you and Fergus will be able to attend. There will be a supper afterward. We hope you can share this joyous occasion with us.

Affectionately,
Marjabelle

RESPONSE ENCLOSURES

For many years, the inclusion of a response card in a wedding invitation was considered something of an insult; it implied that the receiver did not know enough to reply to an invitation. As it turns out, in our busy world, many people, whether they know they should or not, fail to take the time to reply to invitations. So the response card has become acceptable for the bride who wants a well-planned wedding. If you feel the card will offend anyone, you may simply not enclose one in that invitation. Remember, however, that there is no correct way to check on guests who have not responded. You usually must plan the wedding and reception as though everyone who has not responded were attending.

Response cards can be purchased from a stationer or the printer who prepares the invitations. They should, as nearly as possible, match the invitations.

ANNOUNCEMENTS

Persons who are not invited to a wedding, either because they live far away and could not attend or because the number of guests invited to the wedding was very limited, are usually informed through an announcement that the wedding has taken place.

Announcements, similar in shape, size, and form to invitations, are always sent after the wedding has taken place. They can be sent after any kind of wedding, even an elopement.

The wording of an announcement is only slightly different from that of a wedding invitation. The year is always included, and the name of the church may be left off, although the city and state where the ceremony took place is included. Announcements usually take this form:

Mr. and Mrs. Robert L. Gibson
have the honour to announce
the marriage of their daughter
Kelly Jane
to
Mr. Mark John Barker
on Tuesday, the second of June
Nineteen hundred and seventy-seven
Council Bluffs, Iowa

When a wedding is very large or the persons being married are prominent and want to keep out reporters and other uninvited persons, church cards are sometimes issued with the invitations. They are on paper and in a type style similar to the wedding invitations and should read:

Please present this card
at Visitation Church
on Saturday, the sixth of June

A more old-fashioned but thoughtful custom at a large wedding is another kind of church card that ensures that favorite relatives and family friends will be seated near the front of the church. These cards may be printed, or you may purchase suitable cards to write on or use the bride's mother's informals. Such cards consist of a handwritten note

(46)

saying, "Within the ribbons," "Bride's reserved section," or "Groom's reserved section." Guests should carry them to the wedding and hand them to an usher.

ADDRESSING THE INVITATIONS AND ANNOUNCEMENTS

Printed or engraved invitations and announcements usually come in two envelopes and often come with tissue to protect the printing. The inner envelope is ungummed, and it should be placed inside the larger envelope so that writing faces the flap. You may include the tissue or omit it; if included, it should be placed over the printed or engraved part of the invitation.

Correct way to handle
the double envelope

The envelopes should be addressed on a day when your handwriting is at a peak—or perhaps someone in your family or a close friend with particularly lovely handwriting would be willing to address them for you. For a fee, you can also hire a professional calligrapher to address them for you. Only black or dark blue ink should be used to address the envelopes. Abbreviations should not be used, except for *Mr.* and *Mrs.* If an envelope is sent to a husband and wife, it should read:

Mr. and Mrs. Bruce James Stewart
522 South Tremont Street
Trenton, New Jersey 08608

The inner envelope should repeat the last name only:

Mr. and Mrs. Stewart

An invitation should never be addressed to "Mr. J. Johnson and wife," nor should it say, "and family." If you want to include children under eighteen in the invitation, on the inner envelope, write:

Mr. and Mrs. Stewart
Nancy, Amy, Rodney

Dates or fiancés of single guests, roommates, children over eighteen, and children living apart from their parents should be sent separate invitations. When invitations are sent to children over eighteen and parents who live together, the outer envelope should read:

Mr. and Mrs. Robin John Faull
Miss Kathy Ann Faull

The inner envelope should read:

Mr. and Mrs. Faull
Miss Faull

Invitations issued jointly to sisters over eighteen should read:

Misses (or The Misses) Julie and Amy Stewart

The inner envelope should read:

Misses (or The Misses) Stewart

Brothers over eighteen are addressed the same way, only "Messrs." or "The ·Messrs." is substituted.

The outer envelope to a widow is addressed:

Mrs. John Flint Brown
(her deceased husband's name)

The outer envelope to a divorced woman should read:

Mrs. Flint Brown

(a combination of her surname and her former husband's surname, unless, of course, she has taken back her maiden name)

A return address should be included on the envelope. It can be written on the back flap or the upper left-hand corner of the envelope. The engraver can also engrave it in raised letters with no ink on the back flap.

A nice touch to any wedding invitation is to use a pretty, decorative postage stamp on the envelope. Check your post office to see what is available. When you buy the stamps, you might also have an invitation weighed, just to be sure it will go through the mails with the regular postage. Occasionally, elaborate invitations on heavy paper require extra postage—a source of embarrassment to the bride who didn't check first.

AT-HOME CARDS

A card announcing the married couple's new address is usually enclosed with the announcement, or the address may be printed on it. It is a nice way of notifying friends of your new address. An at-home card reads as follows:

> *At home*
> *after the eighth of June*
> *1255 North Lake Shore Drive*
> *Chicago, Illinois 60680*

Or it could read:

> *Mr. and Mrs. Harold John Brown*
> *after the eighth of June*
> *1255 North Lake Shore Drive*
> *Chicago, Illinois 60680*

CARD FILE

When you send your invitations, set up a card file of the guests' names and addresses so you are ready to record their replies to the invitations and keep a record of their gifts. Make out a 3 x 5-inch card for each guest and file them alphabetically. As the guests reply to the wedding, note their acceptance or regrets. A different color ink for each is especially helpful. When a gift arrives, pull out the card of the guest who sent it and note in detail what the gift is and the store from which it was sent, in case you find you must return it. As you write a thank-you note, make a notation on the card, along with the date the note was written. A very large wedding guest list might be most efficiently handled by using several file boxes, or you might use one file box and several sets of dividers. Whatever you do, don't leave this organization to the last minute, or you may never know who sent what gift and who has responded to your invitation.

ACKNOWLEDGING A WEDDING INVITATION

An invitation to a wedding and a reception must be answered as soon as possible, usually within a few days of the receipt of the invitation.

The response to a wedding reception invitation is handwritten in the same language as the invitation itself. If the invitation is an informal note from the mother, the guest writes an informal note back to the mother. If the invitation is formally worded, the response should be handwritten as follows:

Mr. and Mrs. Edward John Peterson
accept with pleasure

(*or* regret that owing to their son's graduation they must decline)

Mr. and Mrs. Richard D. Erickson's
kind invitation for
Saturday, the first of June
at eight o'clock
at Midland Country Club

The receipt of a wedding announcement does not require an answer, just as it does not obligate one to send a gift. A note of best wishes and congratulations and a present may be sent if that is your pleasure. It is entirely up to the receiver's feelings.

Handling Family Problems

Divorce, which is common today, can throw a wrench into the bride's plans if she does not take into account the feelings of those involved when she plans the wedding. Although there are some rules to follow with regard to divorced or separated parents, the best rule is to remember that people's feelings are more important than rules. These feelings should always be taken into account when a woman whose parents are divorced or separated marries.

WHO GIVES THE WEDDING?

If the bride's father is on fairly amicable terms with his ex-wife, he generally gives the wedding, pays for all or half of it, and is treated as the official host with the bride's mother acting as the hostess. However, their duties and seating arrangements may be arranged so they do not, for example, sit next to each other during dinner or stand together in the receiving line.

More likely, if the parents have been divorced for many years, the mother will give the wedding. In this case, she is the official hostess and the father, if he attends the reception, is an honored guest. He would not necessarily stand in the receiving line, and he would not sit at the bride's table.

If divorced parents give the wedding jointly, they may issue the invitations and announcements jointly. If the mother has remarried, her new formal married name and the father's name both may be used on the invitations, or the mother's name alone may be used. If the parents and stepparents are all on friendly terms, they may choose to issue the invitation in both sets of names.

GIVING THE BRIDE AWAY

If the bride has any relationship with her father, he gives her away. If her father is not living or she has had no relationship with him for several years, she may ask an uncle, family friend, older brother, godfather, or stepfather to do this honor. In this case, when the man is asked who gives the bride in marriage, it would be especially gracious to respond, "Her mother and I do."

SEATING AT THE WEDDING

The mother of the bride sits in the first pew on the left side of the aisle. If she has remarried, her husband sits with her. If neither parent has remarried and they are on friendly terms, the parents may choose to sit together in the first pew at the wedding. If the father of the bride has remarried, he and his wife, if she attends the wedding, traditionally sit in the third pew, although you may seat your father in the second row if you prefer. If the bride has a warm relationship with her father's wife, she is invited to the reception, although she has no official function. Seating arrangements for the groom's parents if they are divorced or separated are similar.

DIVORCED PARENTS AT THE RECEPTION

Treatment of divorced and separated parents at the reception can also pose some problems. If your parents do not want to receive the guests together, there is nothing unusual about a father who bows out of the reception line and mingles with guests as they arrive. If your father is sharing the expenses or paying for everything, ask him to join the receiving line; he should also be given a special parent's table or place of honor in the seating arrangements. Two parents' tables usually provide the best way of doing this. Divide the honored guests and relatives among your two parents' tables. If both parents and stepparents issue the wedding invitation, all four may stand in the receiving line.

Sometimes the father will prefer not to attend the reception at all, even though he has given you away at the wedding. Usually when this occurs, the father gives a reception or wedding supper to which his friends and family are invited. The bride and groom attend this reception in their wedding clothes immediately after attending the mother's reception. Occasionally the father's reception is held on another day. The bride and groom dress according to the degree of formality; they do not wear their wedding outfits.

FAMILY OPPOSITION TO YOUR MARRIAGE

Saddest and most difficult is when one or both parents oppose the wedding for any reason.

Before you announce and plan your wedding, try to resolve these differences, perhaps through a neutral, respected third person who can talk to all parties involved.

If your parents oppose the marriage but are still willing to give you the wedding and will happily appear at the celebration, you can go ahead with your wedding plans. If the opposition is bitter to the point where your parents will not give the wedding, you have no choice but to be married quietly, perhaps at a friend's home. Your parents should be given an opportunity to attend a quiet wedding—or even to give it right up to the last minute, should their feelings change.

Finally, a note to all family members: a wedding is for the bride and groom. It is a time to set aside family differences and behave as pleasantly to each other as possible. Just as the tactful bride and groom take into account estranged parents' feelings, the parents should make this a time to be especially considerate of their children's special day.

10

Organizing the Reception

The minute you know you are getting married is the time to start planning your reception, particularly if the wedding and reception are going to be large. In every community, it seems there is one baker who does the loveliest wedding cakes or a florist who seems to specialize in the type of flower arrangements you like, and if you want to be sure of obtaining the services of these people, don't waste any time contacting them once you know you are going to be married.

Almost all the services required at a reception can be prepared by specialists, or you can have a do-it-yourself reception, as described in chapter 11.

THE FIRST STEP

Decide on the formality of your wedding, the kind of reception you want, the number of people you will invite. Once you've lined up your attendants and drawn up a guest list, you should have a pretty good idea of the number of people who will be present at the rehearsal dinner, wedding, and reception.

Draw up a list of all the services you think you will need at your reception. Basically you will need a place in which to hold the reception, a florist, a baker to supply your wedding cake and any other baked goods you may choose, a photographer, musicians or some facilities for music, possibly a caterer to provide food, and possibly a supplier of liquor or champagne, depending upon the place you select for your reception and the services it offers.

Before you buy anything, contact as many suppliers as possible for general estimates and a rundown on their services. Tell them what you have in mind and try to be open to any suggestions that they may make. Ask about package deals and tipping policies. For a set price per person, some restaurants will provide everything from finger sandwiches to a seven-course meal. Other restaurants or catering services will charge for everything from the number of waiters required to the bottles of liquor consumed.

Once you have found a place that offers the services you need at a price you can afford, make an appointment to see the person in charge. Take in your detailed list and discuss everything you will need. Be sure to ask for a written estimate of costs and liabilities in case the reception must be canceled; it is your only protection against unnecessary costs. Reserve the room or rooms and food, liquor, and other services you need at this time. Specify, in writing if possible, the exact services you want— cloth rather than paper tablecloths and napkins, glass rather than plastic glasses, no coat racks in sight, all signs off walls, plumbing and pipes covered with screens or drapes, tablecloths to cover the bar table, good china and silverware, all chairs in good condition, and so on.

THE FLORIST

The florist, too, should be lined up as early as possible. Careful thought should be given to the selection of a florist; if possible, find one who specializes in weddings. Or better yet, ask friends for the names of florists they have used.

Flowers are traditionally carried by the bride and her attendants, and worn as boutonnieres by the groom, his attendants, and the father of the bride. The mothers and grandmothers of the bride and groom are usually given corsages, although this is no longer mandatory. The bride and her attendants may also wear flowers in their hair.

Flowers may also be placed on the altar, or used to mark off the church pews. Jewish couples are married under a *chuppah*, a canopy symbolizing their future home, and flowers are frequently used to decor-

(55)

ate it. Some *chuppahs* are constructed entirely of flowers. When selecting flowers for the ceremony, remember that you are the focal point of the service and keep flowers simple enough so they don't detract from the event.

If you are being married at home, in a club, or in a hotel, flowers will be especially important, as they can form the backdrop replacing a church altar and can be used to mark off aisles. Flowers banked against a fireplace, bay window, or wall between two windows especially contribute toward a lovely setting. Aisles can be created with standing urns filled with greenery and a few flowers strung with ribbon. For an evening wedding, flowers are often used with ribbons and candles. An arbor or archway constructed with greens and flowers makes an especially nice focal point at a garden wedding.

You will also need flowers for your reception. A bouquet will be needed for the service table and the bride's table. If you are having a formal dinner, you may want small floral arrangements at each table. Be sure table arrangements are low, especially at the bride's table.

The Number and Season of Flowers

Flowers can become a major cost at a wedding if you use great quantities of them. Remember that many lovely effects can be created with greenery and a small number of flowers. Another way to eliminate unnecessary expense is to choose flowers that are in season. A thoughtful florist will point out which flowers are in season at the moment. Generally, Easter lilies are traditional in early spring. White tulips and lilac are also lovely and in season for a spring wedding. White peonies are frequently used in May, and roses throughout the summer. Even daisies, simple as they are, form a charming bouquet combined with lacy ferns and baby's breath. White chrysanthemums are a lovely fall and winter flower. Careful thought should be given to the selection of flowers, for they add much to the beauty and romance of the ceremony.

Once you have selected a florist, make an appointment to meet with him to discuss your overall needs. Most ideal is to meet with him at the reception site and at the place where your wedding will be held.

The florist will have one or more books showing flower arrangements that you can look through, and he will also be able to supply you with countless suggestions. Making weddings beautiful is his business.

Flowers for You and the Bridesmaids

Your bouquet should be white or pastel. Many brides have their bouquets made of silk flowers, which they can use later in their homes. Dried flower arrangements have also become popular. Some brides carry only one flower or a few flowers with a prayer book, but as a rule, the bride's bouquet is the most elaborate.

The flowers carried by the bride and her attendants should be coordinated in mood and color, and the maid of honor may carry different flowers from the bridesmaids. The fabric and style of dresses and the theme of the wedding should be taken into account when planning the flowers. An old-fashioned garden bouquet, for example, is lovely for a summer wedding where the bride and attendants are wearing organdy, but it is out of place at a formal wedding when everyone is wearing moiré or another formal fabric. Keep the bouquets fairly small, so you can all be shown off in your lovely dresses.

Flower girls carry a small basket of flowers or rose petals to strew about the church, or a nosegay. If you plan to have the flower girl scatter rose petals, check to be sure the church doesn't have rules against this.

(57)

Mothers and grandmothers always appreciate flowers that indicate their importance in the wedding proceedings. They can be corsages or flowers to pin on their purses. Cymbidium orchids and roses are good choices; other traditional flowers include gardenias, violets, daisies, or a mixed flower arrangement.

Frequently the bride wears a corsage with her going-away outfit. If you plan to do this, have it built into your bouquet so you can remove it just before you toss the bouquet.

Flowers for the Groom and His Attendants

The groom and every man in the wedding party—including both fathers —wear boutonnieres in their left lapels. The groom's boutonniere is frequently taken from the bride's bouquet—a single white rose, a sprig of stephanotis, or a sprig of lily of the valley. White carnations are the most popular flower for boutonnieres for the men. The ring bearer should be given a boutonniere as well, and grandfathers also appreciate them.

Flowers for the Reception

Aside from the flowers you and your attendants carry, the most important and noticed flowers will be those at your reception. Tell the florist you want a masterpiece. Flowers are not necessary at either end of the receiving line, but banks of ferns or potted palms are a nice touch. Remember, too, that potted plants can be used to hide any minor eyesore in the room where the reception is held. You may also want a few banks of ferns or potted palms at the spot where you plan to take formal pictures.

If you have planned a formal dinner or seated buffet, consider small centerpieces of a few flowers attached to a candle or a candelabrum flowing with greenery and ribbons and a few flowers.

The bride and her attendants may arrange their bouquets on the bride's table to make the centerpiece.

A small nosegay is often used to top the wedding cake. If you plan to do this, remember to tell the baker to insert a small water container about the size of a shot glass on the top of the cake. The nosegay is placed in it after the cake is assembled, usually right before the reception. Greenery and rose petals are sometimes scattered on the tablecloth around the cake, and the bride's bouquet should be placed in plain view on the table while photographs of the cake-cutting are taken.

Other Services a Florist Offers

Florists who are wedding specialists frequently can supply a kneeling cushion for the bride and groom, a canvas runner for the aisle, standards for large flower arrangements at the altar or reception, candleholders and candles, white satin ribbon to rope off the front pews, a canopy between the sidewalk and the church door, a cushion for the ring bearer, and a special bouquet to be presented at the foot of the statue of the Blessed Virgin Mary—a tradition at many Roman Catholic Weddings.

What the Florist Needs to Know

Aside from the obvious and already mentioned things, such as the theme of your wedding, a description of your dress and veil, and your attendants' dress, the florist needs to know when and where to deliver the flowers. This may seem a minor point, but many a wedding has been delayed because of confusion over the arrival of flowers. Safest and most convenient is to have flowers for you and your attendants delivered to the church about two hours ahead of the service. The florist will usually show up to help the bride, bridesmaids, and flower girls with their flowers and to instruct them on just how to carry them. If he doesn't, remember that flowers should always be carried in their most natural position, that is, with the stems down. If a bride's bouquet is full at one end and tapers on the other, the tapered end is the bottom of the bouquet.

Flowers for mothers, grandmothers, and other honored guests are usually delivered to their homes, usually early on the day of the wedding.

A form that can be copied and given to the florist to supply him with the information he needs to plan lovely and appropriate floral arrangements for your wedding and reception is on pages 162–65 of the bride's organizer.

As a final note, if you use a lot of floral arrangements at your wedding, put someone in charge of dispensing with them after the reception. You may want to give them to close friends or attendants or send them to an old people's home or some charitable organization. Hospitals rarely accept cut flowers anymore, but it is nice to offer them to someone who can appreciate their fleeting beauty.

THE BAKER

Wedding cakes are traditionally tiered and frosted in white, possibly with some pastel touches. They are made of white cake, but brides who have other preferences are following up on them more and more often these days. Also, the top tier of a wedding cake is often made of fruit cake that can be frozen and saved for future anniversaries.

You can choose either a professional baker or someone in your community who has built a reputation for making fabulous cakes—as long as you choose someone with expertise in making wedding cakes. Many communities have a bakers' association that will refer you to one or more bakers. The women's page editor or food editor of your local newspaper may also be able to recommend someone.

Plan to meet with the baker to discuss your color and style preferences. Some bakers have sample books that you can use to select the cake. When you meet with the baker, have in mind the theme of your wedding, the number of guests so the baker can determine the size of the cake, and any other baked items you may want, such as small pieces of cake that guests can take home with them.

The tradition of the tiny bride and groom atop the wedding cake seemed to be on the wane for a few years, but has now returned to popularity. Second choice for many brides is a small arrangement of flowers, and if this is your preference, be sure to so indicate to the baker so he can make appropriate arrangements.

Make arrangements for the cake to be delivered to the reception site several hours before the big event. Most multitiered wedding cakes are not brought to the reception already assembled, but need to be put together on the spot. Be sure to allow enough time. The cake can form the centerpiece of the bride's table, or it can be placed on its own special table.

Many weddings feature small pieces of cake (either fruit or pound) in special souvenir boxes for the guests to take home. This is often called groom's cake, and it is said that a single woman who places it under her pillow will dream of the man she will marry. The cake, which may be square, rectangular, triangular, or heart-shaped, is baked especially for this purpose and cut to the size of the box. The tiny white boxes may be plain or stamped with the name or initials of the bride and groom and the date of the wedding and tied with ribbon. The boxes are arranged on a small table near where the guests exit. Some bakeries or caterers will prepare these all made up, or you can order the boxes and cake and assemble them at home. If you do not wish to go to the expense of supplying the boxes, do have a supply of cellophane bags ready for your guests to take their cakes home in.

THE PHOTOGRAPHER

A phenomenon of the wedding day is that the bride and groom remember less about it than anyone else. Perhaps this is one reason that photographers play such an important role in this romantic, glamorous event. Weddings truly are too beautiful to entrust to memory—and photographs will be especially treasured by all who are involved in the wedding.

Wedding photography is expensive. If you decide to save money by asking a friend to take pictures, be very sure that you will be happy with the results and that your friend and his or her camera are totally reliable. It is probably wisest to engage a professional wedding photographer to record your special day.

Friends who have been recently married can suggest qualified persons, and you should talk with several photographers before you finally settle on one. Ask the photographers to supply references and check on them to be sure that you are hiring someone who is reliable. Meet with the photographers to look at their samples. Make sure that the photographer for your wedding will be the person whose samples you like. Ask for a written confirmation of price and the number of photographs in black and white and color that you are obligated to buy. Discuss with the photographer the kind of pictures you want and where you expect them to be taken to be sure that you both agree, so there will be no last-minute mix-ups or unmet expectations.

Basically, there are several kinds of photographs that you will want of your wedding: your official bridal portrait, formal portraits of you and the groom during the ceremony (if permissible), formal portraits of you and your wedding party and close members of your family, and candid pictures, usually taken during the reception.

Your Bridal Portrait

Your bridal portrait is taken at the time of your last fitting or, occasionally, right before the ceremony. Many photographers come to the store to photograph you during your last fitting. If yours does, he or the store will probably supply some type of bouquet, but you might want to check on this in advance. Other photographers will prefer to photograph you in their studios, and some will come to your home, if that is preferred.

A bride's make-up is always best understated but well applied. Use your regular daytime make-up if a color portrait is made and perhaps slightly heavier make-up if a black-and-white portrait is taken. The photographer can probably give you some advice on this, but you should stay with the make-up you are most comfortable wearing, so that your wedding portrait will look natural. For specific hints on looking your best for the bridal portrait, see chapter 13.

Photographs of the Wedding and Reception

Insist on the most unobtrusive, natural photography possible. Modern photographic equipment makes it possible to record your wedding and reception without the use of flashbulbs and from a distance, so that the ceremony is not disturbed and guests are rarely aware of the photographer's presence.

Formal portraits of you and your wedding party, except for a few at the altar immediately after the ceremony, as well as family pictures, should be taken after everyone has gone through the receiving line. It is rude to keep guests waiting while you have your picture taken.

The "posed" pictures you will want as keepsakes will probably include:

You and your groom
You alone with your mother
You alone with your father
You with your mother and father together
You with the groom's parents
You with your attendants in a group and in individual pictures
    with each attendant
The groom with his attendants

The wedding party, usually at the altar

You and the groom with grandparents and any favorite relatives or honored guests

Traditional pictures taken at the church include:

Each attendant, including flower girl and ring bearer, as he or she waits to walk down the aisle (especially nice if you give these photographs as remembrances from you).

Your mother coming down the aisle with an usher

The groom's parents coming down the aisle with an usher

Wedding party at altar

You and the groom exchanging vows, exchanging rings, and kissing at end of ceremony

Some of the "candid" pictures you will want to capture include:

You putting on your veil, perhaps with your mother's or a bridesmaid's assistance

Informal shots of you and your attendants just before the ceremony

Informal shots of you and your father leaving for the church

Random shots of guests going through receiving line (Ask a close friend to point out special persons to the photographer at this time.)

Your first dance with the groom, and dances with your father and father-in-law

Cutting the cake and feeding it to each other

Toasting each other

Toasts offered to you by others

Tossing the garter (Your groom removes it first. Be graceful about this and help him by moving it below your knee—this will also help to avoid the suggestion of "cheesecake" that comes when your wedding dress is pulled up around your thigh.)

Tossing your bouquet

Telling your parents good-by after the reception

You and the groom leaving in car

As a final reminder, be sure the photographer has the address and time of the wedding. Call him to remind him again of the exact time a few days before the wedding.

THE MUSIC

Music is probably the single best mood creator you can have at a reception. It sets the tone. Slightly fast, happy music will probably make the receiving line move more quickly, and it will get the reception off to a dazzling start.

If you can possibly afford it, hire musicians for this special occasion. A pianist or an accordianist is a good choice, since you need only one; three to five musicians is ideal, and, of course, you can have a full dance orchestra if that is your choice. If you hire a band or an orchestra, be sure the contract has an "in-person" clause to ensure that you get the same musicians you heard in rehearsal and not substitutes.

The union requires that musicians play for a specified time and then take a break, so if possible, hire a musician to play during the break in order to maintain the festive mood.

The music can be as varied as you wish—it certainly should be light, festive, and in keeping with the occasion. If there will be dancing, you may want to select some contemporary pieces, but an extended period of this music could drive away some of the older guests.

If you cannot afford musicians, you can use recorded music. Especially useful for this purpose is taped music that can be played continuously.

On page 166 of the bride's organizer you'll find a form to help organize the music for your reception.

BEVERAGES FOR THE RECEPTION

The drinks you serve at your reception are a matter of your personal taste. Traditionally brides and grooms toast each other with champagne, but the toasts can be made with punch, either alcoholic or nonalcoholic, or mixed drinks or wine. The cost of liquor will be a major part of the reception expense, so you will want to buy it carefully and wisely.

Whether you are charged by the bottle or the drink by the caterer or reception hall, you should estimate the amount of liquor or drinks that will be required. Estimating the number of drinks to be served will also help you determine the number of people required to tend bar, the amount of mix to order, and the amount of glasses and ice to provide. Plan on three to four drinks per person over a three-hour period. One bartender will be needed for every fifty people served.

The least expensive way to buy liquor for your wedding reception is to purchase it yourself and have it delivered to the site of the reception. There are a few things to keep in mind when doing this.

Champagne

The traditional wedding beverage is purchased by the fifth or in even larger sizes. Call several liquor dealers to get estimates on the most economical purchase. Champagne glasses vary in size from three to six ounces.

Imported champagne is the most expensive; domestic champagne costs slightly less. After you get your liquor merchant's advice on the champagne he recommends, buy one or two bottles and try them yourselves, perhaps over several quiet dinners. The variety in taste and dryness in champagnes makes it necessary for you to sample them to know where your taste lies.

Wines

More and more couples today are choosing to serve wine along with or instead of champagne. You can make your selection from among thousands of wines, and you will probably want to follow the advice of a good wine merchant before you make your final selection. It is also a good idea to sample the wines you are considering.

Generally, white wines are served with white meat and red wines are served with red meat, with rosés being the in-between wines that go well with everything. Wines produced in Europe, and especially in France, are more expensive than domestic wines. The year a wine is gathered is known as the vintage, and wine gathered during a good year is also more expensive than other types of wine.

White wines are chilled slightly, and red wines, which should also be opened and allowed to breathe for about two hours prior to serving, are served at a cool room temperature. If you decide to serve wines, ask a friend or bartender to be sure the wines are properly handled.

Liquor

You can serve a variety of mixed drinks or you can limit the choice to one or two. Whiskey sours, screwdrivers, and Bloody Marys are ideal for a brunch or early afternoon reception. Another advantage to serving a limited selection of drinks is that they can be served from punch bowls.

In large quantities, liquor is most economically bought in quarts or half-gallons. If you are buying by the case, you can also buy by fifths. Twelve fifths make up a case. When buying cases of liquor, ask the dealer for a discount. At 1½ ounces per drink and three drinks per person, 1½ cases should serve 100 people. Buy whatever mix you will need for punch or mixed drinks, and plan to have some extra around for children and people who don't drink alcoholic beverages.

On pages 167–68 of the bride's organizer is a form to help you choose and order the right amount of beverages for the reception.

OTHER ACCESSORIES FOR THE RECEPTION

An assortment of paper accessories is needed at a reception. Be sure to order matches, paper napkins, place cards, and cake boxes if needed. These items are usually printed with the names or initials of the bride and groom and the date of the wedding. Gold or silver ink are traditional, but you can select any color you like. Paper that requires printing should be ordered eight weeks before the reception.

CHOOSING A HOSPITALITY COMMITTEE

Receptions are for people. Too often a bride becomes so carried away with her starring role that she forgets that everyone at the wedding is her guest. Remember that you and your groom should circulate among the guests, thanking them for coming and making sure that they are having a good time.

Often the most awkward moments at a wedding reception are the early ones, when the wedding party may be off having their pictures taken or when some people are going through the receiving line while others are merely waiting before or after going through it. An excellent way to ease these awkward moments is to ask several friends or couples to serve as your hospitality committee. To determine how to station your friends so they can be most useful, go with your mother to the place of your reception and map out a floor plan showing where you will put the buffet tables, receiving lines, cake and refreshment table, and guest book. This will make it easy to station your hospitality committee where they can be most helpful.

If the reception is large, you will want to ask friends to serve in shifts. Call or write brief notes asking people if they will pay you the honor of assisting at your wedding. Tell each one exactly what his or her duties will be and when he or she will be needed. Having definite plans and duties for all assistants ensures that your reception will go as smoothly as possible, whether it is held at home or elsewhere.

A sample note from your mother outlining a helper's responsibilities might read:

Dear Mary Lou and Bob,

Thank you for your kindness in offering to assist at Bob and Jackie's reception Friday, the 16th of May. Jackie and I would like you to take charge of the guest book from 4 to 5 o'clock. I hope this time meets with your approval. If not, please let me know so that we can make any necessary changes. Janet Young will be in charge of the assistants' list at the reception, so you may want to seek her out when you arrive. We are looking forward to seeing you and, again, thank you very much.

Affectionately,
Jane Stewart [bride's mother]

A bride could also write such a note. After the reception, be sure to write thank-you notes to each person who helped.

Among the duties you might wish to delegate are the following:

1. Taking charge of the bridal guest book
2. Passing champagne, lemonade, cold water to waiting receiving line (be sure there is a table nearby to put glasses on before guests go through the line)
3. Cutting and serving the wedding cake
4. Pouring and serving the coffee, punch, or tea at buffet table
5. Taking careful charge of the bridal gift book and table, including gift cards.
6. Passing sandwiches, canapés, mints, and other food

7. Keeping the buffet tables and plates filled
8. Assisting in the kitchen if kitchen help is limited
9. Greeting guests at each door or entrance to the home or garden or outside near reception room at public halls in hotels
10. Showing guests where to place coats
11. Inviting guests to see the wedding gifts
12. Assisting with decorations, the night before or the day of wedding
13. Passing the rice or paper rose petal bags
14. Circulating among the guests, introducing themselves and introducing others
15. Passing the boxed pieces of wedding cake
16. Removing empty plates and cups after guests have been served
17. Introducing the bride's mother to any guest she might not know
18. Taking care of the groom's parents, introducing them, and serving them

11

A Do-It-Yourself Reception

A do-it-yourself reception is especially meaningful because you can have all the personal touches you want.

It does take time and effort, but this isn't a project that you need do entirely alone. Enlisting the aid of willing friends and relatives is always easy when a wedding is involved. Do remember to buy small gifts for people who contribute to your reception.

THE FIRST STEP

If the wedding and reception will take place in your home, the first thing you should do is plan where you want the ceremony to take place. Then plan where you will want the main activities of the reception— cutting the cake, toasting—to occur. Draw up lists of everything you will need—tables, flowers or plants for a backdrop for the ceremony, serving pieces, a coat rack, extra chairs. Many of these things, including silverware and dishes, can be rented for the day or borrowed from friends.

Plan the menu. Unless the wedding is very small, most do-it-yourself receptions are casual buffets. Small sandwiches and punch are ideal, although you can also serve a more substantial buffet of ham or roast beef and side dishes, along with mixed drinks.

Even if you are handling everything yourself, you might want to allow yourself one luxury. Hire a bartender and one or two persons to serve and pass the food. The bride doesn't serve the food at her reception, even if she has prepared it all, and the use of a few people to take over this task will add a professional, elegant note.

THE WEDDING CAKE

If you decide to make your own wedding cake, the "recipe" that follows is excellent and can be done with a minimum of effort.

> 6 frozen vanilla layer cakes (17 ounces each)
> 1 16½-ounce can vanilla frosting or your favorite homemade white frosting
> Wedding ornament or flowers for the top

Arrange four cakes in a large square on a serving platter. Stack the remaining two cakes on top of each other to form the second layer. The already frosted cakes need only a light touch-up with frosting to join the seams. Canned frosting and a pastry tube can add the finishing touches of fancy trims. Just before serving, position a decoration on the top of the cake. Serves 40.

Other recipes are available for the traditional round, multitiered wedding cake. When you serve this kind of cake, keep a damp cloth handy so you can clean the knife from time to time. To begin cutting, remove the top tier. Cut a circle about two inches in from the outer edge. Working from this circle out, make vertical cuts about an inch apart until the entire ring is sliced into wedge-shaped pieces. Remove these pieces of cake to individual serving dishes. Cut another circle two inches

SIZE OF TIER (ROUND)	NUMBER OF SERVINGS
6 inches	16
8 "	30
10 "	48
12 "	68
14 "	92
16 "	118
18 "	148

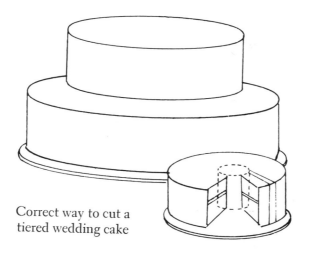

Correct way to cut a
tiered wedding cake

from the edge and repeat the above procedure, which will leave a core of cake when the tier is finished. When you have cut one tier, begin to cut the next tier in the same way. The chart above shows the number of people served by each size tier of cake.

MAKING YOUR OWN PUNCH

For convenience, you may want to have a nonalcoholic and an alcoholic punch. The following recipes are excellent. To open champagne, hold the bottle in one hand and turn the cork with your other hand. Be sure to hold the bottle pointing away from your face. Gradually work the cork out.

NONALCOHOLIC WEDDING PUNCH

    4 cups sugar
    4 cups water
    2 cups strong black tea
    6 6-ounce cans frozen lemonade concentrate, undiluted
    2 6-ounce cans frozen orange juice concentrate, undiluted
    2 46-ounce cans pineapple juice (5 cups)
    2 cups cut-up fresh strawberries and juice (or 16 ounces frozen
        strawberries, thawed)

(71)

1 gallon water
2 quarts dry ginger ale

Make syrup by boiling sugar and 4 cups of water ten minutes. Add tea and fruit juices. Chill two to three hours. Add remaining ingredients. Pour over block of ice in punch bowl or over ice cubes. Makes 60 to 70 servings.

CHAMPAGNE WEDDING PUNCH

10 fifth bottles brut champagne
¾ cup cognac
¾ cup yellow Chartreuse
¾ cup Cointreau
3 fifths sparkling water
  Sugar to taste
  Slices of fresh orange, lemon, and pineapple
  Fresh mint

Mix all the liquids, adding sugar to taste. Set a ring of ice in a punch bowl and pour in the mixture. Garnish with the fruit slices and mint sprigs. Makes about 70 servings.

CHAMPAGNE PEACH PUNCH

2 12-ounce cans peach nectar
1 6-ounce can frozen orange juice concentrate, undiluted
3 cups water
¼ cup lemon juice
⅛ teaspoon salt
3 large bottles California champagne, well chilled

Combine all ingredients except champagne and chill well. At serving time, put in punch bowl over small chunk of ice or ice cubes. Add chilled champagne. Makes about 42 servings.

CHAMPAGNE ORANGE PUNCH

2 6-ounce cans frozen orange juice concentrate, undiluted
1 6-ounce can frozen lemonade concentrate, undiluted

1½ quarts ice water
1 large bottle California champagne
Orange slices

Dilute orange juice and lemonade concentrates with ice water in punch bowl. Just before serving, add well-chilled champagne and garnish with orange slices. Makes about 24 servings.

THE FOOD

The recipes that follow will each make enough sandwiches to serve 100 people. Simply cut down the quantity of food or increase it if you are serving fewer or more people or want to have an assortment of foods.

TEA SANDWICHES

8–10 loaves thin-sliced bread (or 12–14 loaves regular-sliced bread)
3 pounds butter or margarine
2 quarts mayonnaise

Fillings:

PINEAPPLE/HAM: Mix 4 pounds coarsely ground cooked ham, 4 pounds soft cream cheese, 4 1-pound 4-ounce cans crushed pineapple, drained.

HAM SALAD: Mix 6 pounds coarsely ground cooked ham, 4 cups minced celery, 3 cups pickle relish, 4 cups mayonnaise, 4 tablespoons Worcestershire sauce.

HAM AND CHEESE: Mix 3 pounds coarsely ground cooked ham, 3 pounds coarsely grated cheese (processed cheddar), 2 cups undiluted evaporated milk, 3 cups pickle relish, 4 teaspoons dry mustard, 2 teaspoons salt, ½ teaspoon pepper.

CHICKEN SALAD: Mix 16 cups diced cooked chicken (6 4-pound stewing chickens or 4 32-ounce cans boned chicken), 6 cups diced celery, 4–6 cups mayonnaise.

TUNA SALAD: Substitute 16 6½- or 7-ounce cans tuna (16 cups) for chicken in chicken salad recipe above.

EGG SALAD: Substitute 80 chopped hard-cooked eggs for chicken in chicken salad recipe.

SLICED TURKEY, HAM, OR BEEF: Use 2 30-pound, or 4 18-pound turkeys

(73)

(or a 12–16-pound canned ham, sliced, or roast beef, rolled rib, about 40–50 pounds).

CREAM CHEESE: Mix 8 pounds soft cream cheese with one of these: 4 pounds crumbled crisp bacon; 7 cups chopped stuffed olives; 4 cups chopped nuts.

SLICED MEAT: Hot or cold: To serve cold sandwiches, use 6 heads of lettuce and one of the following meats. To serve hot sandwiches, substitute 14 quarts of gravy for lettuce. Roast beef, rolled rib, weight (bone-in) : 40–50 pounds.

SMOKED TONGUE: 40 pounds.

ROAST TURKEY: 2 30-pound birds.

. For attractive ways to cut sandwiches, consult your favorite cookbook.

Sandwiches can be spread and assembled (borrow large trays from relatives and friends if necessary) the morning of the wedding, then covered and refrigerated until serving time. If this is your plan, make sure you have plenty of help. You don't want to be exhausted for your own wedding. It's a good idea to make whatever you can in advance and freeze it.

ADDITIONAL TOUCHES

Mints and nuts add a delicious and relatively inexpensive touch to the reception. Four pounds of each should be adequate, along with sandwiches and a punch, for a reception of 100 guests.

If you serve liquor at the reception, it's always a good idea to provide coffee for your guests near the end of the reception. For 100 guests, you'll need about three pounds of coffee, one quart of cream, and one pound of sugar. Borrow or rent a large urn to serve it in.

Remember to use your imagination in planning your reception. Such things as candles, greenery, and pretty tablecloths can be bought or borrowed for very little, and they can provide an atmosphere that makes the wedding especially memorable.

Although you can plan to hold the wedding outdoors, make contingency plans just in case the weather does not cooperate. If you do have the wedding outdoors, consider renting a large colorful tent to add to the atmosphere of gaiety.

12
Wedding Attire

All little girls at one time or another have a fantasy of themselves float-ing down a church aisle in a long white dress and an even longer white veil—the most elegant and formal of wedding outfits. By the time your wedding day arrives, you may or may not have decided to fulfill each detail of this childhood fantasy. Many brides do wear formal regalia to their weddings. Other brides wear less formal but equally beautiful wedding gowns. And many brides today are choosing simpler wedding dresses or even street clothes in which to be married. Regardless of the degree of formality of the dress you choose, you should look your loveliest on your wedding day.

Depending upon the kind of wedding—formal, less formal, or even informal—that you and your fiancé have planned, there are a few guidelines to help you both choose your wedding clothing.

Of course, the most important outfit at any wedding is yours, the bride's. The attendants' dresses and the dresses worn by the mothers may echo the style of the wedding dress, but they never rival or even equal it. When it comes to dresses, the bride's is the loveliest, most romantic, and most glamorous. You should take the time needed to find and select a wedding dress that you love, one that will fit you per-fectly and flatter you completely.

TYPES OF WEDDING DRESSES

For a very formal wedding, held during the day or at night, the bride wears a full-length white wedding gown, usually of a formal fabric such as velvet, satin, peau de soie, taffeta, organdy, silk, or chiffon. Your veil may be either long or short, and you may have a train if you like.

A less formal church wedding offers the widest range of possibilities for dress. You can wear a long white dress and veil, or you can wear a dress, suit, coat and dress, or dress with jacket. You may wear any veil that is flattering to your outfit, but floor-length veils are not usually worn at a less formal wedding, and the wedding dress does not have a train.

If you are married very quietly in a judge's chambers, a clergyman's study, or a registrar's office, you should wear street-length clothes and an appropriate head covering, if you choose, which may have a small veil. Your outfit may be white or any pastel color that is especially flattering to you.

CHOOSING YOUR WEDDING GOWN

Choosing your wedding outfit is probably the most important thing you will do to set the mood and tone of your wedding. It is a very personal decision that you alone should make, although you may want your mother, maid of honor, or another close friend to come along to offer advice.

Bridal gowns are purchased in two seasons: spring/summer and fall/winter. You try on the store's sample gowns, but your gown is especially ordered and fitted to you. So that your outfit can be ordered and fitted in time for your wedding day, you should allow eight to twelve weeks between the day you choose your wedding gown and veil to the day of your wedding.

White is the traditional color for a wedding outfit, and this includes very delicate shades in pale, pale pink or blue, ivory, and light beige. The color you select will depend upon your own coloring; dark-skinned brunettes look good in ivory or beige, and fair-skinned blondes may find they look better in a white-pastel or pure white gown. De-

(77)

pending upon their skin tones, black brides and redheads can wear many different shades of white.

Popular fabrics for a winter wedding dress are lace, crepe, taffeta, peau de soie, satin, brocade, and velvet. Lovely summer fabrics are organza, chiffon, linen, piqué, eyelet, and dotted swiss.

Call a department store or specialty store to make an appointment to look at its wedding dresses. At the time you make the appointment, discuss with the clerk the formality of your wedding and how much you can afford to pay for a wedding dress. That way, you can be shown only those dresses that are in your price range, and you won't have to torture yourself by falling in love with a wedding dress that is far beyond your means. Wedding dresses usually cost between $140 and $300, although you can spend far more if you choose a very expensive fabric or a designer label. Headpieces cost between $40 and $200. In addition to these expenses, you will probably have to buy matching shoes, gloves, and lingerie to complete your wedding outfit.

On the day of your appointment, plan your make-up so it is as similar as possible to the way you would like it for your wedding day. Take along or wear a pair of shoes of the approximate height you would like to wear with your wedding dress. Be sure your hair is attractively arranged. In short, look as lovely as you can for this shopping day.

Wedding gowns come in many styles. If you are seeking a period mood for your wedding—Victorian, for example—mention this to the person who waits on you. If you really don't know the style of wedding gown you would like, feel free to say so and try on as many gowns as you like. This is too important a decision for you not to find the gown of your dreams.

HEIRLOOM GOWNS

Some brides are lucky enough to have a dress that has been handed down through the family, perhaps through a grandmother or great-aunt. If such a gown is offered to you, and it suits your taste and looks marvelously flattering on you, by all means wear it. On the other hand, if you really don't like the dress or its style doesn't suit you well, graciously decline to wear it. Your choice of a wedding dress is highly personal and you should not feel any pressure to wear one you aren't fond of. You can tell the well-meaning relative who offers the dress that you have always wanted your own wedding dress and have planned it to the most minute detail. If you decide to wear an heirloom dress, have it fitted to you if necessary.

CHOOSING YOUR HEADPIECE

Second in importance only to your gown is the headpiece you choose to set it off. Headpieces, like wedding dresses, vary in formality and are chosen to complement the dress. The one you pick should match exactly the shade of your dress and generally should be made of a similar or complementary material. If you know you want your headpiece made of matching fabric, ask the bridal consultant who takes your order to order an extra half yard of fabric that matches your dress. She may be able to recommend someone to make the headpiece, or you can find someone who can do it. Some brides make their own headpieces. If you can sew or enlist the aid of a talented friend, you might want to design your own headpiece and veil.

A headpiece should be chosen because it flatters you. Take your hair style, face shape, and figure into consideration. Of course, you will want to try on various headpieces with the dress you have chosen.

Tall, oval-faced women can wear almost any style of headpiece. Persons with round faces and short women may want to select a headpiece that adds height. A long face is softened by a band or wreath cap and a full, puffy veil. Tiaras are especially flattering to women who wear glasses or have round faces. The Juliet cap is particularly flattering to someone who is a little overweight or is short. It looks best worn with a short veil.

The romantic wide-brimmed hat is most becoming on a medium to tall woman with chin- or shoulder-length hair. It usually goes with a casual wedding dress or a suit or daytime dress.

These style hints are not hard and fast rules. You may find that you look especially good in a mantilla even if you aren't tall and stately. Try on the various styles and choose the one that you love and look beautiful wearing.

Most headpieces come with a veil. The four-yard cathedral veil is generally worn only at a very formal wedding. In fact, this veil often serves as the train on the dress. The chapel veil, three yards long, is perfect for a less formal church wedding where you are wearing a long-

The wreath cap
and puffy veil

The tiara

The wide-brimmed hat

(80)

The juliette cap

The mantilla

(81)

sleeved full-length dress. An elbow-length or fingertip-length veil is lovely with a short-sleeved wedding dress and also shows off a pretty back. Bridal gowns made of synthetic materials like jersey and dressy knits look wonderful with a cascade veil—an almost straight veil from a simple headpiece.

If you plan to dance at your wedding, you may want to order a veil that can be snapped off the headpiece.

YOUR ACCESSORIES

You will probably want a new lacy set of lingerie to wear with your wedding dress. It should be white or a very pale pastel or beige and delicately detailed—the nicest you can afford.

Shoes are dyed to match and are usually chosen in a material that matches or coordinates with your wedding dress. Silk is appropriate with every fabric. Peau de soie or satin works well with a winter fabric. Linen is good for a summer fabric. You can wear a pump or a dressy sandal. Buy your shoes well in advance of your wedding day so you can "practice" walking in them and break them in.

Applying a light coating of sand to the soles of your shoes on your wedding day is extra insurance against slipping as you walk down the aisle.

The rules about gloves are more relaxed these days. Bare arms are no longer cause for controversy, except possibly among grandmothers and great-aunts. Wear the style and length of gloves that look best with your dress, and if no gloves look right, go bare-handed. If you wear kid gloves, they should be silk-lined so you can easily slip off the left one to accept your wedding band. If long gloves are worn, you can slit the ring finger of the glove.

PRESERVING YOUR GOWN

You may want to have your dress preserved so it can be offered to a good friend or sister, or cut up to make a christening gown. A professional cleaner will be able to advise you on preserving your gown; the cost is about $55.

CHOOSING YOUR ATTENDANTS' DRESSES

Your attendants' outfits are chosen at the same time or shortly after your dress is selected. They, too, take about eight weeks to order, and then fittings are usually required. On pages 157–60 of the bride's organizer you'll find forms to record the necessary measurements.

Their dresses should be similar in style, mood, and fabric to your dress. They need not be the same fabric, but if your dress is peau de soie, you won't want your attendants wearing organdy. Also, if you are wearing a Victorian-style dress, you will want your attendants' dresses to capture the mood your dress sets.

Although your bridesmaids must accept your choice of a dress for them, you want each woman to be dressed in a style that is flattering to her, so take your attendants' figures and personalities into account when you choose their dresses. Also take their coloring into account when selecting colors.

Your attendants will probably be paying for their own dresses, so show consideration for cost when you choose their dresses. Remember that they also may have to buy shoes and accessories. A small deposit is usually required when the dresses are ordered, and the full amount is paid after the final fitting.

Bridesmaids' dresses should be the same style, but they may vary in color. They are usually in colors, although occasionally one sees an all-white wedding party. The maid or matron of honor may wear a slightly different style. The flower girl should wear a dress that harmonizes with the rest of the wedding party.

ATTENDANTS' ACCESSORIES

The attendants' shoes should all be alike. If possible, have them dyed at the same place so they will be exactly the same shade. Attendants wear the headpiece you choose, and it should complement their dress. If you want your attendants to wear jewelry—something small and conservative such as pearl button earrings or a small pin—consider presenting the jewelry as your gifts to your bridesmaids. Otherwise, attendants should wear no jewelry, with the possible exception of small earrings or a ring.

YOUR JEWELRY

A bride wears very little jewelry—usually only an heirloom piece or something appropriate that the groom has given her. Pearls are always appropriate, as is gold. If you wear your engagement ring, remember to switch it to your right hand for the ceremony, and if your engagement ring is one that interlocks with the wedding band, remember to give it to the groom before the ceremony. Watches are never worn by any member of the wedding party—this is a day when, symbolically, time does not matter. Bracelets are not usually worn by a bride either.

YOUR TROUSSEAU

Most brides today do not shop for a closetful of clothes, but you should fill in with anything you will need for your wedding trip or the parties that surround your wedding. If you will be moving to another part of the country, buy whatever clothing you will need before you are married. Your clothing should also be suitable to your new life style. Whether you will become a sophisticated urban wife who does a lot of entertaining or a casual working wife, plan your wardrobe to suit your new life.

WEDDING OUTFITS FOR THE MOTHERS

The mothers of the bride and groom are officially members of the wedding party, and they dress accordingly. Even if most of the guests will be in street-length clothes, it is correct for the mothers to wear long dresses if they prefer. The mothers should, however, get in touch with each other so that their dresses will all be the same length. The mothers no longer must choose dresses that are in keeping with the style and color theme of the wedding party. Most important is that the mothers choose dresses they like and will enjoy wearing. All white and all black are not usually worn by the mothers of the bride and groom, but prints of these colors are acceptable.

(84)

The later in the day the wedding is held, the dressier the mothers' gowns can be. Before six, they generally wear short, dressy cocktail-style clothes with matching headpieces. After six, long dresses can be worn. The day of the "mother-of-the-bride dress" is gone. Mothers may choose anything from an elegant wool dress to an elaborate and brightly colored evening gown. The mothers generally do wear head-pieces.

THE GROOM AND HIS ATTENDANTS

Most of the men in the wedding party—including the groom—will appreciate some hints on what they are expected to wear. Wedding clothes for men are usually rented these days. This is an advantage, since it ensures uniformity among the groom, fathers, and attendants. The wedding clothes for the men vary with the time of day and degree of formality of the wedding.

Traditional attire for a formal evening wedding during winter includes the black tailcoat and trousers with satin stripes, a white single-breasted waistcoat, a dressy evening shirt with wing collar and cuff links, pearl studs instead of buttons, and a white tie—always the traditional formal bow tie. Ideally, patent leather tie shoes or pumps are worn with black dress socks. A high silk hat and white gloves are optional.

Contemporary attire for a formal evening wedding includes a contoured long or short jacket with matching trousers, a wing-collared shirt, and vest or cummerbund and bow tie.

For an elaborate formal daytime wedding, the groom and his attendants traditionally wear gray cutaway jackets or Oxford jackets and dark striped trousers, gray waistcoats that may be single- or double-breasted, and white shirts with wing collars or turndown collars. A black-and-white striped tie is worn with a wing collar, and a gray or black-and-white checked four-in-hand tie is worn with a turndown collar. Accessories are gold, pearl, or white studs and cuff links, black dress socks, and plain-toed black shoes. A black silk topper and gray suede gloves are optional.

Contemporary attire for a formal daytime wedding includes a contoured long or short jacket in black or gray with striped trousers, wing-collared shirt, and a gray vest if desired. Colors may also be worn to the formal daytime wedding—deep shades of burgundy, rust, green, and blue

(86)

are fine for fall or winter weddings; pastels and white can be chosen for spring and summer weddings.

For a formal summer wedding, the groom traditionally wears a white dinner jacket and black, satin-striped trousers, black cummerbund, white formal shirt with turndown collar and French cuffs, simple links and studs, black socks and shoes, and no hat or gloves.

For a semiformal daytime wedding, the groom and his attendants wear gray sack coat or stroller jacket with dark striped trousers, and a gray single- or double-breasted waistcoat. A white shirt with turndown collar and French cuffs with conservative gold cuff links are worn. The tie is gray-and-white striped or a checked four-in-hand. Gold, black, or white studs are worn in the shirts. Black socks and plain black leather shoes complete the outfit unless the groom wishes to add the optional homburg and gray suede gloves. An alternate outfit is a formal wedding suit such as rental agencies carry in a choice of colors and styles, worn with a matching or contrasting cummerbund, dressy bow tie, and vest. Black socks and black leather shoes are worn with most colors; black socks and white shoes with lighter shades.

At a semiformal evening wedding, the groom and groomsmen traditionally wear black dinner jackets, matching trousers, black vests and cummerbunds, and suitable accessories. In summer, a white dinner jacket is worn. For a contemporary look the men may choose to wear formal suits in darker colors for fall and winter and in lighter colors for summer and spring. They should wear matching trousers and a bow tie to match a vest or cummerbund.

At an informal wedding, the groom and his attendants wear solid dark business suits in black, navy, or dark gray, conservative white shirts with a four-in-hand tie, and black shoes and socks. In summer, he and his attendants may wear white jackets with gray trousers or navy jackets with white flannel trousers, or white suits.

The attendants and the father of the bride always wear exactly what the groom wears. If the father of the groom will stand in the receiving line, he should wear what the other attendants wear.

Rental outfits should be ordered about four to six weeks before the wedding. The rental shop may supply mail-order fitting cards so that out-of-town attendants can be measured at a local shop. A day or two before the wedding, the men in the wedding party should be fitted to their outfits.

It is especially important that all the men understand the fine points of fitting a man's suit so that all members of the wedding party will truly look identical. Here are some hints:

The shirt collar should hug the neck. The shirt sleeves should extend no more than one-half inch beyond the jacket sleeve.

Jackets should button easily and not pull in any way.

Trousers should touch the vamps of shoes.

Black shoes and socks are worn with dark clothes; light-colored shoes and pastel or light socks are worn with light trousers.

Finally, if the men are wearing light trousers, ask your groom to remind them not to wear colored underwear and to wear briefs rather than boxer shorts.

The ring bearer can wear a dress suit with long or short pants in navy blue or white in summer. Sometimes an outfit identical to that of the groomsmen can be rented for the ring bearer.

13
The Bride's Beauty Care

The life of a bride-to-be usually becomes hectic shortly after she announces plans for her future life. As the wedding day approaches, many brides find they have trouble stealing the extra half-hours for beauty care that they always assumed was their prerogative as the beautiful bride. The amount of time you have for hair and nail care seems to diminish in relationship to the time that is taken up with prenuptial festivities. Too often, the bride awakens on her wedding day to find herself harried, her hair not quite as beautiful as she would like, and her nails in need of a manicure. Careful planning can eliminate these problems and make your wedding day the restful, joyous, and beautiful occasion it should be.

Plan to save a few extra minutes a day for yourself right from the beginning. Especially as your wedding day nears, excuse yourself from the parties at a decent hour so you can get the rest you need.

Experiment with your hair and make-up well in advance of the wedding, particularly if you are planning any major changes. Above all, think twice about major changes. Don't cut your hair short if you've worn it medium-length for ten years, unless you were planning to do so anyway and you are very confident that the new style will suit your life style and personality.

If you are planning a major change in make-up or hair, plan it carefully. Shop around the stores to see what is available in make-up, study the magazines, listen to your hairdresser and make-up expert, but do your own thinking. Make changes that you want—you are the one who will have to live with them. Even in these days of liberation, most brides-to-be make at least a routine check with their fiancés to be sure that they won't hate them with short hair or thinner eyebrows. It may be that the very trait you're planning to change is one that he finds especially dear about you; in that case, you may want to keep things as they are for your wedding day.

This is one time in your life to splurge. Treat yourself, if you can afford it, to a facial the week of or day before your wedding. Consult with a make-up expert several weeks in advance of the wedding. If he or she suggests a new make-up and you approve, buy the necessary materials and use them every day so that you are comfortable and confident with your make-up on your wedding day.

If you are thinking about a haircut or a permanent, take care of this at least a month before the wedding. (You may have to go back for a trim or a prewedding set, but you will be adjusted to the new style.) Here are a few basic rules to follow about such major changes:

1. Have the changes done by experts; this is no time to trust the judgment of friends or relatives.
2. Talk to your hairdresser about your wedding and the look you want.
3. Condition your hair before you get a permanent.
4. Think twice about getting a permanent if you color your hair. Sometimes this creates problems that take a long time to correct, and you don't want to be worrying about this and your wedding.
5. Have your hair cut before you get a permanent. It rids your hair of any split or dead ends and gives it the shape it needs for the permanent.
6. Condition your hair regularly for a month after a permanent.

Every bride wants to look her loveliest for her wedding portrait. It is, after all, the official record of your appearance on your wedding day. Apply your make-up carefully, and manicure your nails even if they won't show—it will give you confidence. Here are some specific tips for looking your best:

Make-up Tips for Your Wedding Portrait
1. Use foundation or medicated make-up to cover flaws or dark circles under the eyes.
2. If your skin has a shine, the photograph will have white spots,

so powder over make-up generously to a matte finish. Also powder exposed skin on neck and shoulders.

3. Use pastel eye shadow. Deeper shades tend to make the eyes sink into the face, and frosted eye shadows give a white cast.
4. Draw a line above the eye in a soft-colored eye-liner pencil.
5. Do not pluck eyebrows in a thin line. Use a brush to fill in color on brows, nothing heavy.
6. False eyelashes can be worn if they are natural-looking. Don't bother with them, though, if you have never worn them.
7. Apply cheek color in a soft shade, being careful not to get it too far down past your nose.
8. A soft pastel lipstick photographs best. Don't use a pearlized shade, or your lips will look white in the photographs.
9. Spray your hands with hair spray and pat your hair all over.
10. If you are wearing an ivory dress, it might give a yellowish cast to your skin. Stay away from beige tint make-up and use a pink one instead.

By the week of your wedding, you should have gotten all the experimenting out of your system and be ready to sit back and do little but look beautiful.

If you are planning to have your hair done the day before or the day of the wedding, your appointment should have been made early at a time that is convenient for you.

Your make-up supply should be well stocked and only waiting to be applied by you or an expert.

Your nails should be manicured by you or a manicurist the day before the wedding. You can always patch up any last-minute chips the morning of the wedding. (If a manicurist does your nails and you elect to use a pale shade of polish, be sure you have a matching bottle for home use.)

The day of your wedding should be one in which you leisurely make yourself as beautiful as possible.

14

For the Groom Only!

Because the groom has far fewer prewedding responsibilities than the bride, he can be the person who sometimes spirits her away from the hectic activity that inevitably surrounds her as wedding plans proceed.

This is a time to be especially attentive to the woman you have chosen. Plan a few quiet romantic dinners alone so you can maintain the rapport that led you to this stage of your lives. Too often, couples get so caught up in the wedding preparations and festivities that they barely have time alone before the big day. If a party is planned in your honor for 8:00 P.M., take a few minutes to have a quiet drink with each other in a favorite bar or pub. If an early evening cocktail party is planned for you, sneak away to a quiet dinner alone afterward. Remember, you are the guests of honor at the festivities, so it is entirely proper for you to leave first.

Few grooms would forget to tell their brides how beautiful they look on their wedding day were it not for the nervousness that often besets them. Make a point of complimenting your new wife frequently during the day—after all, she has taken care to look her loveliest for you. When the inevitable compliments come to her from guests, be the first to agree. A wedding day is no time for modesty over your selection of a wife.

In addition to attentiveness to the bride, the groom has a few small tasks to perform.

His major task is planning the wedding trip that he and his wife have decided to take. Make any transportation arrangements and make sure you have hotel reservations well in advance. The first day of your married life is no time for things to go wrong in the travel department.

Choose your attendants and plan and order their outfits, based on the degree of formality of the wedding. Also order your outfit for the wedding.

Arrange for your attendants' accommodations, if they live out of town. If they will be staying in a hotel, arrange to pay their bills.

The parents of the groom usually give the rehearsal dinner, so talk with your parents about the party. More information on this is in chapter 19.

With your fiancé, meet to talk with the clergyman who will perform the wedding, meet with the musicians if you are interested, and, of course, take her to select and then pick up the wedding rings. Needless to say, all these obligations provide the perfect opportunity for festive lunches or dinners together.

Put your financial affairs in order. Be sure your wife will be covered by your insurance if necessary. Open any new checking or savings accounts you will need as a couple.

Buy gifts for your best man and ushers. If you are giving your bride a wedding gift other than her rings, arrange for the gift. Sometimes a woman is given heirloom jewelry from the man's family, so you may want to discuss this with your mother.

Make a date with your fiancé to pick up the marriage license. Make sure all other necessary documents—passport, birth certificate, records of blood tests—are in order.

Make plans for your bachelor party if you are giving one.

Plan to pay the clergyman or give the money to your best man. The clergyman should be paid the last time you meet with him, at the rehearsal, or just before the ceremony. Traditionally, he is paid from $10 to $200 depending upon local custom, size of wedding, and your circumstances. A call to the church office's secretary usually uncovers the expected amount. If it doesn't, pay what is comfortable to you. Pay with new bills placed in a sealed envelope with the clergyman's name written on it.

Make any necessary arrangements to move your belongings into your new home. Make arrangements to move your wedding gifts to your new home.

Arrange all transportation required for your wedding day.

During the week of the wedding, there should be only a few last-minute preparations:

1. Recheck all documents, financial arrangements, travel arrangements, and moving plans.
2. Be sure your outfits are ready and will be delivered to your home the day of the wedding.
3. Meet with your ushers and best man to remind them of the time and date and any duties they have.
4. Pack for your wedding.
5. Show up at the church an hour before the ceremony—certainly before your bride. You may want to have the best man call her home to say you are at the church and to determine the time of her arrival, particularly if you are superstitious about seeing her before the wedding.
6. Be sure your wedding certificate is properly signed and stored before you leave for your wedding trip.

The Honeymoon

The wedding trip you and your new husband take after the wedding is one of the best parts of getting married. The tension of the final few days evaporates, the big ceremony is actually over, and you are alone together on a vacation.

Plan a trip that you will both enjoy. It is perfectly O.K. to follow up on an interest you share, but it won't be much fun to go skiing if one of you does not ski. Sit down together to discuss the kind of trip you have in mind. Unless one of you is an experienced traveler, you may want to forgo an adventurous trip to new lands on your first trip together. Are you both active, urban-oriented people? Then go to a country resort only at your own risk, or if you are both sure that round-the-clock relaxation is what you have in mind. Last of all, decide what you can reasonably afford to spend on a honeymoon.

During the planning stages, you should visit the offices of a travel agency to pick up some brochures on areas you think you might like to visit. Then when you start planning the trip, return to the same travel agent. This is one trip that even experienced travelers will want to go smoothly, so the services of a good travel agent will probably be a great help.

Frequently, people do not realize that travel agents do not charge a fee for booking trips; instead they receive their commission from the airline or resort they send you to. Therefore, it is a courtesy to allow the travel agent who has given you advice to at least book the transportation part of the trip. A travel agent who has spent a fair amount of money in long-distance phone calls and wires should also be reimbursed for these expenses.

If you have decided to go to one place and stay for the entire time, check to see if there is a honeymoon package price. Many hotels have special packages even for one or two nights for honeymooners, so it is to your advantage to mention that this is your wedding trip.

Most travel agents will prepare a written itinerary of your trip without your asking. Regardless of how you get it, you should have one, along with any confirmation slips and airline tickets. With everything in writing, there should be no last-minute confusion about time schedules, costs, dates, meal plans, and any extras you receive.

What if, with all these precautions, the trip planned by the agent doesn't live up to his or her promises? What if, for example, you were sold the American plan, which includes the meals, but received the European plan, which does not include meals? Misrepresentation is a serious consumer abuse for which you should obtain financial redress from the company that sold you the accommodations. If a settlement cannot be made amicably between you and the agent, file a complaint with your local Better Business Bureau or a consumer protection agency.

Finally, don't try to take off on your wedding trip or even go anywhere very far away on the day of your wedding. You will probably be too exhausted and disoriented, and this may get your entire wedding trip off to a bad start. Instead, plan to stay somewhere nearby in a nice hotel and get a leisurely start to your final destination the next day.

Just be discreet about your plans so you won't be harassed by well-meaning but thoughtless friends who decide to join you on your wedding night.

LUGGAGE

If you're buying new luggage, investigate the numerous kinds before you make a final purchase. The kind of luggage you buy should be suited to your personal taste and your travel needs. If you will be taking vacations in resorts or one hotel, and will fly to your destinations, you will probably find one large Pullman suitcase that can hold up to two weeks' worth of clothes most useful. Another good piece of luggage is a small overnight bag to put under the plane seat.

If you plan to travel by train, particularly in foreign countries, you might do better with two small suitcases, since you may have to carry your own luggage sometimes.

When deciding how much luggage to take, remember the restrictions posed by your ability to carry it and the kind of transportation you usually use. You can take as much as you want if you travel by car or train. Airplanes, however, do have restrictions. Check with the travel agent or the airline to learn what their restrictions are regarding the weight that you can check without extra cost.

PACKING

Packing everything you will need and want over a one- or two-week period is no easy matter. Make a detailed list of everything you will need during your honeymoon. List clothes, personal care and health items, and recreation items (tennis racket, some good books, a game or two, a deck of cards) separately. Then set aside an entire afternoon in which to pack leisurely for your trip.

Open your empty suitcase in front of you on a bed or somewhere else. First pack the heavy items—shoes, electric rollers, hair dryer, books, purses. Wrap shoes in covers or plastic bags, and arrange them heel to toe, preferably against the hinge side of the bag.

Next roll and pack crushable separates—T-shirts, jeans, underwear, and nightgowns. Rolled clothes will not wrinkle if they are packed tightly, and they will move with the give and take of a canvas bag or duffle. Tuck rolled clothes into empty spaces and corners; use them as padding. Next pack crushables that require careful prefolding–evening clothes, dresses, skirts. Lay tissue paper or plastic bags between each item to keep it unwrinkled.

Another clever scheme for packing that takes only a little extra time involves the use of brown wrapping paper or plastic dividers that you can easily make. Buy a sheet of paper and cut pieces slightly longer than the length of your suitcase. The long ends will form handles that you can use to lift the layers of clothes and other items in and out of the suitcase. Use a pen to mark on each piece of paper what you have packed in it. Use general terms, such as "underwear," "dresses," and "first night" for the things you will want to get to as soon as you arrive somewhere.

(97)

If you are traveling somewhere by train or plane and will be separated from your large luggage, plan to carry a separate overnight case to ensure that you will at least have the basic things you need when you arrive. Luggage does arrive late even for honeymooners. Pack a nightgown; your beauty and health needs, including your contraceptives; make-up, expensive jewelry, and your camera in the case that you plan to hand-carry. It will relieve a lot of tension if your luggage is temporarily lost.

SPECIAL SERVICES AND TIPPING

If you want any special services—a bouquet from the groom, champagne, or any special food—you have only to order them when you make your final travel reservations. Remember that most honeymoon packages include either flowers or champagne, and many include both. Check this before ordering anything separately.

Almost all hotels of any size offer many special services, such as room service for food, dry cleaning and laundry, a house doctor, a concierge or ticket agent who can arrange for theater tickets or tours, bellhops who take your luggage to and from your room, and a doorman who greets you and removes your luggage, generally into the hands of the bellhop. Since it is your honeymoon, just relax and take advantage of the services, remembering that tips are required somewhere along the way to compensate the people who wait on you.

The doorman is tipped $1 at arrival or departure for loading your car and 25¢ to 50¢ each time he hails a cab for you or gets your car.

The desk clerk is the next person you come into contact with. He does not receive a tip, but if you are going to pay with a credit card, you should tell him when you arrive.

The bellhop who carries the bag to your room should be tipped $1 to $2 depending upon how much he does for you.

The concierge or ticket broker need not be tipped anything, since he takes his commission from the tickets or tour he sells you.

A waiter who brings anything from room service—which can vary from predinner drinks to complete meal or a late-night snack—should be tipped no less than 50¢ and generally is tipped 15 percent of the bill. Tell him when you want him to return to pick up the tray, or, if you do not want to be disturbed, place the tray outside your door.

The woman who cleans your room each day should be left $1 per day for her services.

In the hotel dining room, you tip as you would at any restaurant or night club. If the maître d'hôtel arranges a better table for you or gives you any extra assistance, a tip of $1 to $2 is required. If he only checks your reservations and shows you to your table, no tip is expected. Waiters receive 15 percent of the total food and drink bill. The headwaiter—the man who takes your order and explains the French on the menu to you—receives a 5 percent tip.

If during your stay you have cause to complain about noise or something in the room, call the assistant manager, who runs the front desk. Only if he does not offer assistance should you call the manager.

If you need something special—mending supplies, extra blankets, or ice, for example—call the housekeeper. She is also the person to call if you leave something in the room and notice it when you are 100 miles away.

Always allow enough time to check out. Generally half an hour is enough. If you will not actually be leaving until after check-out time, you may be able to have the time extended, or you can check your luggage with the bell captain until you are ready to leave.

Above all, enjoy your wedding trip. If you've gone to a resort that offers many activities, take advantage of them. If you're visiting another country or a part of the United States you've never seen before, take time to explore the surrounding countryside. Leave lots of time for long, romantic dinners à deux, but also leave some time for each of you to be alone. The togetherness of a honeymoon is, after all, artificial, and it can even start your marriage off badly if you fail to relax and enjoy your new husband or wife *and* your surroundings.

16
Wedding Gifts

Wedding gifts are expressions of people's pleasure and joy in your marriage. They should be accepted in the same spirit in which they are given—even if you do get three identical casseroles and an atrocious dish that your great-aunt Minnie has been saving for you for twenty years.

If your wedding is large, you will receive many gifts, which means that you will have to devote a fair amount of your prewedding hours to the receipt and care of the gifts, to say nothing of writing thank-you notes.

All in all, your wedding gifts should give you much pleasure for many years to come, and they will, if you organize yourself properly to receive them and follow a few simple procedures for ensuring that you mostly receive gifts that match your taste and wants and needs.

As soon as possible after your wedding plans have been announced, plan to register your gift preferences. You should register at a major department store, preferably where you live and in a town where most of your guests and family live. If you wish, you may also register your gift preferences at camping, sporting, antique, plant, or aquarium shops or any other shop that carries your gift preferences.

Before you can register, however, you will have to give careful thought to the kinds of things you want to use in your new household. Generally, brides register preferences for linens (colors, patterns), china and possibly everyday dishes, glassware, silverware, and appliances and other large cooking needs. The latter are largely a matter of practicality and what you need.

Generally, too, the bride has no problems choosing linens she wants. But many brides do not know much about selecting dishes, crystal, and silver, although these are purchases that will be used throughout your life and possibly handed down to a child.

CHINA

The word *china* is popularly used for all kinds of dinnerware, although officially it refers only to fine china, which is either porcelain or bone. Fine china is expensive, extremely hard, nonporous, and translucent. Initially white, it is traditionally painted in a wide assortment of lovely patterns. Too often a bride receives fine china and then fails to use it regularly. When you have something so lovely, why deny yourself the pleasure of seeing it regularly on your table? Most chinas are durable enough to be washed in a dishwasher with a reliable detergent.

Other dishes you may want to receive as gifts include:

Earthenware and stoneware, which are available in a large variety of patterns. These dishes are suitable for everything from today's "formal" dinner to the most casual kind of dining. Both kinds of dishes are thicker than china, not translucent, and less expensive. Earthenware is also soft and chips easily. Stoneware is harder and denser and is frequently found only in serving dishes and tea or coffee pots.

Melamine is a practical plastic dishware that does not chip or break. It is light, comes in a wide variety of patterns, and has a lustrous look to it.

Dishes are bought in three ways: open stock, by the piece, and in place settings. Open stock means that the dishes are expected to be available from the manufacturer over a continuing period of time, and you should check carefully to be sure the pattern you select will be open stock. Manufacturers will not guarantee open stock, however, and occasionally brides do buy something only to find that it is difficult to replace in a few years. Selecting an old china pattern offers some protection against this. If it is taken off open stock, you can usually find replacement dishes at auctions or through a service that specializes in locating old china patterns.

Dishes that are bought by the piece are bought, as you might expect, one at a time. You pay for the saucer, but not the cup; you may buy one dinner plate or six.

A place setting usually consists of a dinner plate, salad or dessert plate, cup and saucer, and soup bowl or butter plate, according to your preference. There is no savings in price if dishes are bought in place settings. Brides usually receive dishes in place settings, but you might pass the word that you prefer to receive individual pieces. That way, you take into account the probability that your tastes will change over the years. If you have a set of dessert plates, it will be easier to replace these with something you like better than it will be to replace place settings.

CHOOSING GLASSWARE

Most brides need and receive glassware. It may take the form of casual glasses, or you may want to register for crystal glassware. There are various kinds of crystal—some of which does not ring when tapped even though it is very fine—and glassware.

Whether you choose a fine crystal pattern or another kind of glassware, you will probably need water glasses, wineglasses, a set of glasses for everyday use, and bar glasses according to your entertaining needs. Especially thoughtful is a present of fine liqueur glasses or brandy snifters.

Crystal glasses may be chosen from among the more elaborate cut-glass patterns, or a simpler pattern may be chosen, depending upon how formally you will be entertaining. Before you select elaborate cut-glass wineglasses or colored wineglasses, remember that wine is usually drunk in plain glasses so the imbibers may observe and appreciate its color.

CHOOSING SILVERWARE

Sterling silverware has become so expensive in recent years that many brides have turned to the equally beautiful silverplate and pewter. There are also many lovely stainless steel patterns; in fact, stainless steel has become the most popular choice of brides today.

Silverware, the term generally used to cover all three kinds of eating utensils, comes in a wide variety of patterns and should be chosen to coordinate with your dishes and glassware.

REGISTERING AT THE BRIDAL REGISTRY

A week or so before you actually register your gift preferences, visit the department store of your choice and pick up brochures on dishes, glasses, and silver to look over. When you are making your final decisions, you may want to visit the store again and ask to see your choices together to be sure everything coordinates.

When you are ready to list your gift preferences, make an appointment to talk with a bridal consultant. Bridal registry is a free service provided by most department stores and many small specialty housewares stores.

Persons invited to your wedding call the store or visit it personally to choose your gift. In stores where you are registered, careful records of what has been purchased for you are kept so that duplication of gifts can be avoided as much as possible.

When a registry is used, there are also no problems in returning or exchanging gifts. A smart bride registers at the main department store in her town, another one where most of her parents' or the groom's parents' friends live, and possibly a small specialized store whose name she can pass along to close friends who make special inquiries about her needs. Try to select gifts in all price ranges.

As gifts begin to arrive, check in every week or so with the registry to be sure that gifts you have received are removed from the list.

The bridal consultant at a bridal registry is usually a person highly knowledgeable in housewares and fine dinner table appointments. If you don't know much about buying these things, this is the person to consult.

DISPLAYING GIFTS

Brides frequently arrange displays of gifts in their homes so they can be viewed by friends and guests. To do this you will need tables on which to display the gifts. In some large cities, a bridal consultant at the department store can tell you where tables can be rented. Or you can build your own, using plywood and wood sawhorses. The tables are covered with white or pastel floor-length cloths, so it doesn't matter what they look like under the covers. White rayon satin is reasonably priced and makes an excellent covering for the tables; you need not even hem it—just buy it longer than the tables and tuck the ends under for a soft effect.

Arranging wedding gifts calls for no small degree of tact. Two lovely but inexpensive potholders shouldn't be placed next to a place setting of your silverware. If you received five crockpots, only one is displayed so the duplication is not obvious. As a rule, a place setting of china, silverware, and glassware is set up once on the display tables.

Remove the giver's cards from presents. Presents of money are noted on a white card, on which the giver's name and the word "check" are written, never the amount.

Some brides do not wish to display their wedding gifts. This is entirely a personal choice, and you as the bride should make your own decision regarding this. But remember that many of your friends and relatives will truly be interested in seeing your presents. If you're moving out of town after your marriage, this may be their only glimpse of your future household.

As you open your presents for display, be sure to keep the boxes they come in, so you can use them later when you pack the gifts to move them to your new home.

INSURING PRESENTS

If you receive many presents, you will need insurance on them. Insurance is a necessity on gifts received for a very large wedding. Any insurance agency will furnish you with a floating policy, which usually lasts three months and covers any damages the presents may receive in shipping. A further precaution, if your wedding has been widely publicized or announced in any newspaper, is to hire a guard for those times when you will be away from the house overnight or when you are attending a party in your honor that has been announced in newspapers. The guard should, of course, sit with the gifts during the rehearsal dinner, wedding, and reception. Contact your local police department or a private agency to find a reliable guard.

EXCHANGING PRESENTS

If you receive very many presents, there will undoubtedly be some duplications. You can never ask someone who gave you a gift to return it —indeed, the giver should never know that his or her gift was duplicated.

Keep the small notices usually posted inside wedding gifts from big department stores to make it easy to return unwanted items. Most practical and convenient to you is to wait until after the wedding to return the gifts. Then you can sort out everything you have received and better organize those presents you must exchange.

Highly personalized gifts that you don't happen to like generally should not be returned, even if they aren't to your taste. If your Aunt Sarah gave you a hideous one-of-a-kind soup tureen, she will expect to see it when she visits you. And to be tactful, you should display it, if only for her visit. But it would be silly to keep a collection of five identical saucepans. Return the four you won't be using.

If a gift arrives damaged from a store and is insured, write the giver so that he or she can make the necessary adjustments for replacement. If a gift arrives damaged and was obviously hand-wrapped by the sender and not insured, simply write a gracious thank-you note as if the gift had arrived in perfect condition.

THANK-YOU NOTES

For every gift you receive, you must send a personal handwritten thank-you note. If your wedding is going to be very large, and if it is impossible for you to keep up with the thank-you notes as you go along, a printed notice indicating that you have received the gift can be sent. Such notes can usually be purchased in the stationery department of any large department store. They usually read as follows:

_____ greatly appreciates
your gift and will take pleasure in writing
a personal thank-you note later.

Thank-you notes are usually written on informals—small sheets of notepaper folded in half. They are printed with your name or monogram, or can be plain white or another attractive color. Notes written after the wedding can be imprinted with your new name.

A thank-you note should be personal. Mention the gift and, if possible, how you intend to use it in your new home. Sample notes follow:

June 6, 1976

Dear Aunt Jane,

You and Uncle Joe were so kind to send Jim and me the lovely silver serving dish. Both of us admire it and look forward to using it at many dinners. We look forward to seeing you at the wedding.

Affectionately,
Jackie

Dear Mrs. Wells,

Our thanks to you for the beautiful vase. It has been given a place of honor on a table in our new living room.

We appreciate your kindness in remembering us with such a truly beautiful gift.

We enjoyed seeing you at the wedding.

Fondly,
Jackie

After you are married, your husband can help you by writing some of the thank-you notes. Whoever is writing simply mentions both of you and signs his or her name. Notes can be dated in the upper right-hand corner or at the end of the note on the left side of the page.

Thank-you notes must be written within three months after the wedding day. People have put a great deal of effort and thought into getting you a present you will appreciate. It is up to you to make them feel appreciated in your thank-you note.

The Wedding Festivities

Aside from the rehearsal dinner, which is considered a part of the wedding itself, there are several types of festivities that surround a wedding. These generally consist of the bride's luncheon, given by her or her attendants; the bachelor party, given by the groom or his attendants; showers given for the bride or the couple, and receptions or more general types of parties given in honor of the couple. A couple never asks anyone to give a party, and generally, they accept the offer of any friend who wants to honor them with a party, unless they have a prior engagement.

THE BRIDE'S LUNCHEON

This gay event, which includes the attendants and mothers of the bride and groom, is usually held the week before the wedding. This luncheon may be given by the bride or by her bridesmaids. It is a relaxed, informal event, and it is also the occasion for a woman to give vent to some of her feminine urges. This is the party that can be colored pink, if that is your choice.

At this party, the bride can give her attendants their gifts and informally review any last-minute plans with them. The traditional cake for this party is frosted pink and a ring or thimble is baked into it. Its recipient is said to be the next bride. This is also a time to show off your trousseau or wedding gifts, if you choose.

Sometimes the bride and groom give their attendants a party jointly. Such a party is usually held in the evening, or it can be a luncheon. It provides a perfect opportunity for the members of the wedding party to get to know each other. When such a party is given, the couple can incorporate as many or as few of the traditions associated with the parties as they choose.

THE BACHELOR PARTY

If the groom chooses, he can plan to have a bachelor party, or his friends may plan one for him. It is usually held the night before the rehearsal dinner or even the night before the wedding, although this custom is waning, and the dinner is now given a week or so before the wedding to ensure good health and alertness on the part of all attending the wedding. The groom's party is traditionally a boisterous one, with many toasts, and the custom of holding it immediately before the wedding is one this writer is happy to see abandoned.

The bride is toasted, usually with glasses that are tossed over the men's shoulders after they are emptied. If this custom is followed, arrangements for it should be made with the restaurant or club where the party is held.

This is the occasion for the groom to present his groomsmen with presents and to make last-minute plans.

GIFTS FOR ATTENDANTS

As soon as possible before the wedding, plan the gifts you want to give your attendants. The best man and maid of honor are usually given slightly more personal and expensive gifts than are the other attendants. The gifts you choose should be a significant reminder of your wedding; frequently they are engraved. Allow a minimum of two weeks for engraving to be completed. Wrap the gifts in pretty paper and ribbons before presenting them.

The maid of honor or best man might receive a gold or silver signature ring or a sterling key ring. Charms, small pins, lockets, and bracelets are excellent gifts for bridesmaids. Ushers will appreciate small leather items, cuff links, money clips, pen-and-pencil sets, or tie tacks.

Especially thoughtful is the custom of giving the mothers and fathers small remembrances of the occasion. They should be small personal items similar to the attendants' gifts.

BRIDAL SHOWERS

Showers are parties usually given in honor of the bride and sometimes given for her and the groom. They are usually afternoon or early evening events; refreshments are served, and decorations, if used, should be light and gay. You may serve tea foods or other light refreshments or a meal.

Since presents are expected from guests at a shower, only close friends and relatives of the bride and groom are invited. Since the same people are frequently invited to attend all the parties, a wise couple keeps the lid on the number of parties given in the bride's honor if possible, or they proportion the guest list for each party among their friends, so that no one is invited to more than a couple of parties. One prospective bride permitted only two showers: one given by a friend of hers, to which her friends were invited, and one given by a friend of her mother's, to which her mother's friends were invited. Everyone was happy.

The old rule that a relative should never give a shower seems to have faded into oblivion. Most women have a loving aunt or cousin who wants to entertain for them, and there is no reason not to do so. Immediate members of the family—sisters and mothers—still do not give showers, although they can have another party where gifts are not expected.

Shower Gifts

Originally intended as small gifts, shower gifts have now come to rival wedding gifts. A considerate bride and hostess will frequently pass the word among potential shower guests that gifts are to be small.

Frequently showers are planned around a gift category; linen, china, kitchenware, bathroom accessories, or personal gifts may be specified by the hostess. If a shower is given jointly for the bride and groom, the presents are always for the household; gifts of a personal nature are never given at such showers. Gifts may be centered around a couple's special interests, such as wine, sailing, cooking out, or fine food.

Thank-Yous

Each person is, of course, thanked when a gift is opened and again when he or she leaves the party. It is nice to write a thank-you note but not necessary unless someone sent a gift and did not attend the shower. Most important, send a personal note to the person who gave the shower in your honor. Thank-you notes should always be hand-written.

OTHER PARTIES

Sometimes parties—not showers—are given to honor the bride and groom. Gifts are not expected; the only obligation is to enjoy oneself. Such parties are frequently planned to entertain out-of-town guests who arrive before the wedding day. They can be breakfasts, lunches, cocktail parties, or dinner parties.

Page 169 of the bride's organizer will help you keep track of all the prewedding festivities.

18
Ceremonies Within Ceremonies

Procedures for wedding ceremonies vary slightly from religion to religion, depending upon whether or not you are having a military ceremony, and on your clergyman's preferences. Your clergyman will, of course, be familiar with the procedures in your religion, but it will help him if you have some idea of the ceremonies that are unique to your religion. It is especially helpful to have a nodding acquaintance with the ceremony if you will be married in a faith other than your own. Then, too, there are a few parts of the wedding service that are optional, so you may want to think about these before you talk with the clergyman.

PROTESTANT CEREMONY

The Christian ceremony developed from the ancient Jewish ceremony, and there is even today a great similarity between the two.

In many Protestant churches, the congregation stands when the bride comes down the aisle and remains standing for all or part of the service. The minister will signal this to the guests.

Two new touches have slipped into Protestant ceremonies over the last few years: the custom of the father kissing the bride at the altar as he gives her away, which is entirely a matter of personal choice, and the ceremony in which the couple kneels to say the Lord's Prayer at the altar near the end of the ceremony. Discuss this with your clergyman, as special arrangements will have to be made if you want this included in the ceremony.

EPISCOPALIAN CEREMONY

At least one of the couple must be baptized in the Episcopalian faith, and by church law the clergyman must be consulted at least three days before the service. This is a formality, since you will have contacted the clergyman as soon as you knew you were going to be married in his church. If both the bride and groom are members of the Episcopalian faith, a Nuptial Eucharist, which includes communion for guests who want to take it, can be held.

In the Episcopalian service, the bride walks on her father's left arm during the processional. A betrothal ceremony takes place on the chancel steps, at which point the father gives his daughter to the clergyman, who in turn bestows her on the groom at the appropriate moment in the ceremony.

The couple, accompanied by their main attendants, go to the altar together for the ceremony. Guests remain standing throughout the ceremony, except when they kneel during communion. (If you are not taking communion, you simply remain seated.)

JEWISH CEREMONY

The Jewish faith has three groups, Orthodox, Conservative, and Reformed, and the ceremony varies depending upon the affiliation of the couple.

A Jewish wedding is often held at the place of the reception—a hotel, private club, or home—although there has been a move back toward holding weddings in synagogues.

Among the Orthodox and Conservative Jews, a couple is married standing under a *chuppah*, or canopy. Usually both parents accompany the bride and groom in the processional, and the parents walk together in the recessional. They stand with their children during the ceremony. The bride stands to the right of the groom. Among the Orthodox and Conservative groups, part of the ceremony is in Hebrew. Near the end of the ceremony, the rabbi blesses a glass of wine, the bride and groom sip from it, and the groom crushes the wineglass under his foot.

In the Reform ceremony, the canopy may be eliminated, as may be the ceremony of crushing the wineglass.

All men attending the Jewish wedding ceremony wear skullcaps or street hats. Skullcaps are furnished at the synagogue for guests who don't have them.

ROMAN CATHOLIC CEREMONY

The father of the bride does not give the bride away. He escorts her to the chancel steps, her maid of honor lifts her veil so her father can kiss her, and she joins the groom at the altar. Some couples are choosing to be greeted by the priest at the vestibule door so he can lead the processional.

Traditional wedding marches, which are secular music, are not allowed in many Catholic churches.

A lengthy nuptial mass, in which the wedding ceremony is incorporated, can be arranged for almost any Catholic wedding. Non-Catholics do not take communion, nor does the non-Catholic member of the couple, if the marriage is mixed.

If there is room, all the attendants step past the altar rail during the ceremony; otherwise only the maid of honor and the best man accompany the bride and groom past the steps. It is customary for the main attendants to be Catholic.

A final touching ceremony within the Catholic wedding occurs when the bride walks back to the left of the main altar to offer her bouquet to the Virgin Mary. She then rejoins her husband for the recessional.

QUAKER CEREMONY

A Quaker wedding is performed during a regular meeting of the congregation. Today's Quaker bride wears the traditional white gown and veil, although it may be fairly simple, in keeping with the bride's religious views. No bridal party is required, although this is becoming common today. The couple enter the meeting together and sit facing the congregation. After the traditional silence, the couple join hands and repeat their vows to each other. The father of the bride does not give her away, and no one officiates at the wedding. The couple may conclude the ceremony with a kiss. After they sit down, the marriage certificate is brought out to be signed after it is read to the congregation. The meeting continues for another half-hour or so until its end.

This ceremony is in keeping with the Quaker view that marriage is a personal and individual commitment, made in the presence of God and friends who witness the ceremony. A Quaker betrothal is announced publicly at meetings several times, usually over a period of three months before the ceremony.

Quaker marriage certificates are treasured documents in Quaker families. Some have been handed down through five and six generations.

A Quaker reception, usually held at the church or in the bride's home, is traditionally kept simple.

EASTERN ORTHODOX CEREMONY

Many Russians, Eastern Europeans, and some Mediterranean people are members of the Eastern Orthodox church, which is ceremonially similar in many ways to the Roman Catholic church but which does not recognize the Pope as the titular head of the church.

Some Eastern Orthodox denominations require that the banns be published three times before the day of the wedding. Sometimes a betrothal service at which rings are exchanged is held.

The processional and recessional are like those of any other wedding. The father of the bride gives her away and then returns to the pew where his wife is seated.

MORMON CEREMONY

Two kinds of ceremonies are performed by Mormons: a religious ceremony in a temple of the church, which is available only to those who meet certain requirements, and a civil ceremony, which may be performed by a clergyman of the church or a civil official. Frequently persons who are married in a civil ceremony are remarried later in the church, after they have met all the requirements.

The vows at a Mormon wedding are taken "for time and all eternity" rather than "until death do you part," as in Christian and Jewish weddings.

CHRISTIAN SCIENCE CEREMONY

Christian Science readers are not ordained ministers, so persons of this faith are married in a Protestant church. If one of the couple is not a Christian Scientist, the couple is generally married in that person's church. If both are Christian Scientists, they should find a clergyman whom they like and ask him to marry them. Protestant clergymen are aware of the restriction and will usually as a courtesy marry a Christian Science couple. Since the couple are not regular participants in this church, the clergyman should be generously paid for his services.

AMISH CEREMONY

The Amish ceremony always takes place on either a Tuesday or a Thursday, and usually in the month of November.

On the day of the wedding, friends, relatives, and neighbors start arriving by 8:00 A.M. At 8:30 the ceremony begins, usually with the chanting of hymns. Then a minister preaches for forty-five minutes, after which a bishop gives the traditional wedding sermon, which lasts for over an hour. When the sermon is completed, the bride and groom are summoned by the bishop to the front of the congregation. After a ten-minute wedding ceremony, the congregation kneels for prayer and a dismissal hymn.

No special wedding attire is worn by the bride or groom; Sunday best doubles as the wedding dress.

The ceremony usually lasts until noon, at which time the backless benches are converted into tables, which are then spread with a feast of delicious food—all prepared the day before. The guests, who may number 500 or more, spend the remainder of the day in feasting and merrymaking.

THE DOUBLE WEDDING

Often sisters or friends who are especially close choose to be married in a double ceremony. The issuance of invitations for such a wedding is discussed in chapter 8.

Each bride has her own maid of honor, although the brides may, and frequently do, act as each other's honor attendants. Other attendants are generally shared, although there may be two sets. If there are two sets of attendants, they need not dress alike, although for appearance' sake, they should be dressed somewhat alike. Similarly, the brides need not wear identical dresses, but one should not be more formally dressed than the other, and their dresses should be somewhat similar in style. All male members of the wedding parties dress alike.

The only other problems unique to a double wedding are the processional and recessional and who does what first. Generally the latter problem is solved by rank—the older bride goes down the aisle first, and she and her fiancé say their vows first, although the ceremony is read only once. (This is only one solution to the problem; brides could draw lots or arrange their order alphabetically.) Generally the older bride stands to the left with her attendants. The younger bride stands to the right with her attendants.

The processional goes as follows: the grooms enter with the clergyman and the best men. Both sets of ushers, paired by height, lead the processional. The female attendants of the first bride, then the bride and her father, follow. The second bride's attendants and the bride and her escort then proceed down the aisle. If the brides are friends, each father accompanies the bride. If they are sisters, another close relative escorts the second bride down the aisle, but the father first gives away the older daughter and then moves to the younger daughter to give her away. At the recessional, the parties may leave separately as they entered, or the couples may leave followed by both sets of attendants.

At the reception, the receiving line also poses some complications. If the brides are friends, two lines are formed in the traditional way, or they can form a joint receiving line, which is set up in this way: mother of older bride, mother of older bride's groom, mother of younger bride, mother of younger bride's groom, older bride and her husband, her honor attendant, younger bride and her husband, her honor attendant, bridesmaids.

THE INDEPENDENT BRIDE

A book on wedding etiquette in this day can hardly ignore the independent woman. She may be a totally liberated woman who wants none of the trappings of a traditional wedding, or she may be a woman who wants all the traditions and customs to surround her wedding. Usually a woman in her thirties, she has worked hard to establish her own career and often plans to continue working after her marriage. She has established her own household, often in a city many miles from her parents, and has stocked that household with her own furniture and household belongings. Do you fall into this category? If so, here are some hints that may help you plan your wedding to suit your independence and keep your parents happy.

First of all, you may pay for any or all of your wedding if you choose, but your parents are still expected to function as the host and hostess. For them not to do so would signify a serious rift between you. Details of who has paid for what are too private to be discussed, and tactful friends won't even inquire. More important, if your mother wants to buy your wedding dress or do something especially nice for your wedding, it would only be emotionally stingy to refuse her that gesture. You can have the kind of wedding you want and still be gracious to your parents.

Where the wedding is held is up to you. If you have been living on your own in a city away from your parents for many years, it is perfectly proper to have the wedding and reception at your home or at the home of a close friend. If you use a friend's home, it is with the understanding that you will pay for everything.

Be sure to invite your mother to all showers and both parents to all parties given in your honor even if you know they can't attend. It will make them feel they are an important part of your wedding.

Gifts sometimes pose a problem for the independent bride, since she already has many household belongings. It is especially important that you register your needs in major department stores where most of your guests live as soon as you have decided to get married. If you have already purchased all your china, for example, simply ask the stores to mark "filled" in that category on the gift list. Remember that no matter how well equipped your household is, you will still want some new things to start married life with. As a matter of fact, you might want to take some time to sort out your belongings before you register for gifts.

The independent bride may have any type of wedding she and her fiancé choose and can afford. Sometimes a couple will find it convenient to share expenses.

One situation that faces the independent bride is her career. After years of assuming responsibility at the office, it wouldn't do to desert your hard-won position by assuming that you have special rights as a bride. You do, but there is a way to assume those rights tactfully. Let your boss in on your engagement as soon as possible. Assure him or her that you plan to continue working, if you do. Discuss the time you would like to take off to prepare for the wedding, and how long you will be gone for the wedding and your wedding trip. Try to plan your wedding around your work schedule, if necessary. Offer to take off extra time beyond the vacation time you have coming to you at your own expense. There is a good possibility that one of the unexpected wedding presents you will receive is a boss considerate enough to give you extra time to prepare for your wedding. Finally, be discreet about your wedding plans—especially if you aren't inviting everyone with whom you work.

If the wedding is small or medium-sized, be sure to send announcements with your new address or at-home cards enclosed to friends and acquaintances who don't attend the wedding. More information on announcements can be found in chapter 8.

As a final note, the independent bride who is fifty years old or over and marrying for the first time usually does not want the traditional elaborate wedding dress and veil. Instead she picks something more suited to her age and personal style. She may, of course, have as elaborate or as simple a wedding and reception as she wants.

SECOND MARRIAGES

Procedures vary slightly for a second wedding only if the bride has been married before. A woman marrying a man who was wed before can have as elaborate a wedding as she chooses, provided it does not violate a rule of her religion.

A bride marrying again does not wear a formal wedding gown and veil, but her dress may be white and she carries flowers. If the wedding reception is formal, she does wear an evening dress. Such a bride is usually not given away, although her father may escort her down the aisle if there is a procession. More often, a second-time bride is married in a quiet ceremony without a processional and attendants. Frequently the ceremony is attended only by close family and friends.

If either one of the couple has children, they may want to make some special provisions for them during the wedding. If the children are old enough, they may light candles before the ceremony or be given some other small role to make them feel a part of the proceedings. Children do not usually act as their parent's attendants if there has been a divorce. They occasionally stand up for a widowed parent.

Friends probably will give wedding gifts, but a friend who was a guest at your first wedding is under no obligation to give a second gift.

WEDDINGS INVOLVING CLERGYMEN

If the father of the bride is a clergyman, he may perform the ceremony, although he does not then give the bride away. The mother may step forward at the appropriate time to do this. The bride is escorted down the aisle by a brother, uncle, godfather, or close male friend.

If the groom is a clergyman, he can be married in the bride's church or, as more often happens, they may be married in his church in a ceremony officiated by his immediate superior or another clergyman of equal or superior rank. The groom may wear regular dress, or formal dress with his clerical collar, a street suit, or his clerical garb. He never wears vestments to his wedding.

ELOPEMENTS AND SECRET MARRIAGES

Sometimes a couple may elect to elope rather than be married in a full-scale elaborate ceremony. An elopement need not signify disapproval on the part of either of the couple's families, but may mean that the couple did not want to go through with an elaborate wedding if that was expected. Most elopements occur with the approval of parents; indeed, it is gracious to let them in on your plans even for the most quiet of ceremonies.

The mother of the bride announces an elopement or a secret marriage with printed or engraved announcements, or she may prefer to write short notes.

Presents may be sent by close friends and relatives.

MILITARY WEDDINGS

A man who is a member of the armed forces may choose to be married in uniform. Most likely, several of his attendants will also be in uniform. A wedding party may also be mixed, with some ushers in uniform and some not. The ushers not in uniform wear whatever is appropriate to the formality and time of day of the wedding. Men in uniform never wear a boutonniere.

Few gestures are as dramatic as the arch of swords that military ushers form as a tribute to the bride and groom. If the ushers are going to form the arch of swords, it is done outside the church door immediately after the wedding if the weather is nice or, if not, at the foot of the chancel steps. If the sword ceremony takes place inside, the ushers line up and at the command "Draw swords" from the head usher in uniform, swords are drawn blade up to form an arch under which the bride and groom walk. Civilian ushers stand in line at attention during this brief ceremony. The ushers return their swords to their sheath, and then escort the bridesmaids in the recessional. (Bridesmaids always walk on the right, since the swords are worn on the left.) If the sword ceremony is outdoors, the bridesmaids walk up the aisle alone or in pairs while the ushers quickly leave by a side door and go to the front steps of the church.

The rank of the groom—and the bride if she is in the armed forces —is listed on the invitations and announcements, as noted in chapter 8.

The Rehearsal

The rehearsal is held, of course, at the church or place of your wedding. The dinner may be held in someone's home or at a restaurant. It can be as formal or as informal as the groom's parents prefer.

Since the members of your wedding party may not know each other, and since there seems to be something inherently tense about a rehearsal, an especially good tactic is to invite the wedding party to your house for drinks and hors d'oeuvres beforehand. Allow the group an hour or so together in this relaxed setting and your rehearsal will go more smoothly. When everyone is already in a party mood, there is less likelihood that the rehearsal will become drawn out.

Brides today stand in for themselves at the rehearsal. After all, no star is ever expected to take the stage without a dress rehearsal. The minister will usually direct the rehearsal anyway, and he will be aware of any special touches you and your fiancé want from previous meetings with you.

WALKING THROUGH THE CEREMONY

A rehearsal is just what it sounds like—a chance for the bride and groom and all the members of the wedding party to practice the steps they will follow during the wedding ceremony. You will probably want two or three walk-throughs to be sure that each person understands what he or she is expected to do. In addition, the attendants (except the flower girl and ring bearer, who are merely told where and when to report to the church) should each be given a list of their responsibilities. If possible, type the lists neatly. These lists can also be passed out and discussed at your house. Following are sample lists:

The Best Man

1. Help the groom dress for the ceremony (which means you must be dressed well in advance yourself).
2. Get the clergyman's fee in a plain, sealed envelope from the groom and deliver it to the clergyman.
3. Remind the groom of the marriage license, airline tickets, and any documents he needs.
4. Get the groom to the church a half-hour before the ceremony, then keep him from going to pieces while waiting in the vestry.
5. Carry the ring in your waistcoat pocket, ready to hand to the groom at the proper moment.
6. Take the groom's gloves as he waits for the bride at the chancel steps (take your own off, too, if it reduces possible fumbling for the ring).
7. Offer the first toast to the bride and groom (at both the rehearsal dinner and reception).
8. Make sure the going-away car is safely hidden away.
9. Help the bride and groom get away from the reception.
10. Return the groom's wedding clothes to his home or to the rental shop.

Maid or Matron of Honor

1. Act as the bride's witness for license and ceremony.
2. Help with her gloves, train, veil, flowers, prayer book, etc., during the ceremony.

Ushers

1. Arrive at the church an hour early.
2. Light the aisle candelabra fifteen minutes before the ceremony.
3. Seat guests.
4. Take down pew ribbons as you come to each new section.
5. Pull the aisle runner into position and pull it back at the end of the ceremony.
6. Walk in the processional and recessional.

7. Return to escort the bride's mother and father and the groom's mother and father out. Then return to take out the rest of the guests an aisle at a time by standing before the aisle to move out.
8. At the reception, each usher takes a turn dancing with the bride and the bridesmaids. They should make sure there are no wallflowers.

It is also especially thoughtful to send notes to the attendants the week before the wedding listing the times and places when you will need them. This is a good time to remind them of any transportation arrangements you have made.

Before the rehearsal, you will probably want to be somewhat familiar with the steps of the wedding ceremony.

Choosing the aisle for the processional and recessional is the first order of business. Usually the center aisle is used if there is one. If there are two aisles, choose the one that is most convenient for you, or use one for the processional and another for the recessional. Note: This may not work if you have white carpet and only want to decorate one aisle.

Once the rehearsal begins, the minister will position everyone at the front of the church as they will stand during the ceremony. Then everyone will practice standing where they should be after the vows are taken, when the recessional is about to begin. As soon as everyone is sure of his or her position during the ceremony, the groom and best man may want to practice entering from the side. While they are doing this, the other attendants can assemble at the back of the church to practice the processional. Everyone stands in the order of his or her scheduled appearance—the ushers, who can enter singly or in pairs; the bridesmaids, who also enter singly or in pairs; the matron of honor; the ring bearer and flower girl, who usually walk together; and finally the bride and her father. Attendants usually pace themselves about six to ten feet apart. The bride waits until the last attendants are about halfway down the aisle, or she may wait until they are all at the altar before starting down the aisle. The processional and recessional should be practiced with music, if possible.

You usually walk on your father's right, taking his arm as you go down the aisle. When you reach the chancel steps, relinquish your father's arm, move your bouquet to your left hand, and wait until the minister asks who gives you in marriage. Your father replies, "I do," or "Her mother and I do," and then takes his place beside your mother in

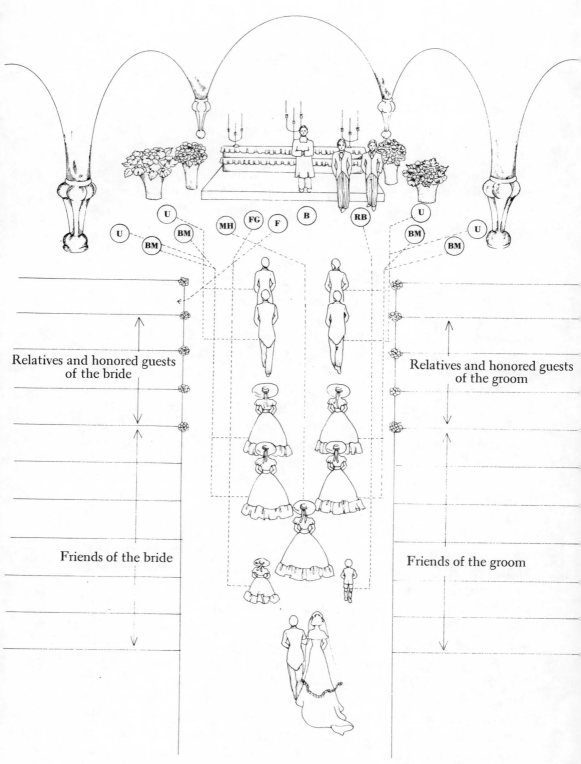

Relatives and honored guests of the bride

Relatives and honored guests of the groom

Friends of the bride

Friends of the groom

The processional: B, Bride; F, Father of the Bride; FG, Flower Girl; RB, Ring Bearer; MH, Maid or Matron of Honor; BM, Bridesmaid; U, Usher

her pew. In Catholic weddings, where the father doesn't give the bride away, he sits down immediately after escorting his daughter down the aisle.

In a Jewish wedding, where the parents often participate in the processional and recessional, the rabbi will offer suggestions.

As you and the groom are about to approach the altar, hand your bouquet to your maid of honor. When the exchange of rings occurs, you separately turn to your honor attendants to get the rings. Hand the rings to the minister.

Generally, the part of the vows that requires a response from you and the groom will be repeated several times during the rehearsal. When the clergyman has pronounced you husband and wife and congratulated you himself, you may embrace and kiss briefly. A passionate embrace is out of place. You are kissed at the altar because the groom traditionally is the first person to kiss his wife. If you and the groom will go immediately to the reception and bypass all guests who might kiss you, you need not even kiss at the altar—although this is a custom that few people forgo. After the embrace, take your bouquet from your maid of honor and start the recessional. If you have a train, the maid of honor may start it as you walk up the aisle. (You might also have someone posted at the back of the church to start your train in the processional.) Walk with dignity during the recessional. The music will be faster than in the processional, and you will be relieved that you actually got this far, but this is no reason to sprint up the aisle. Generally the maid of honor and the best man are paired during the recessional, and the bridesmaids pair up with ushers. The ring bearer and the flower girl generally follow close behind or beside the bride and groom. If you don't want people paired off, it is your decision.

After a couple of run-throughs on the actual ceremony, the processional, and the recessional, everyone should meet at the front of the church to discuss any questions and so the ushers can be briefed on the proper way to seat guests.

SEATING GUESTS

During the rehearsal, the head usher may want to practice seating first the groom's mother and then the bride's mother. For the recessional, the order is reversed, as the bride's parents leave first.

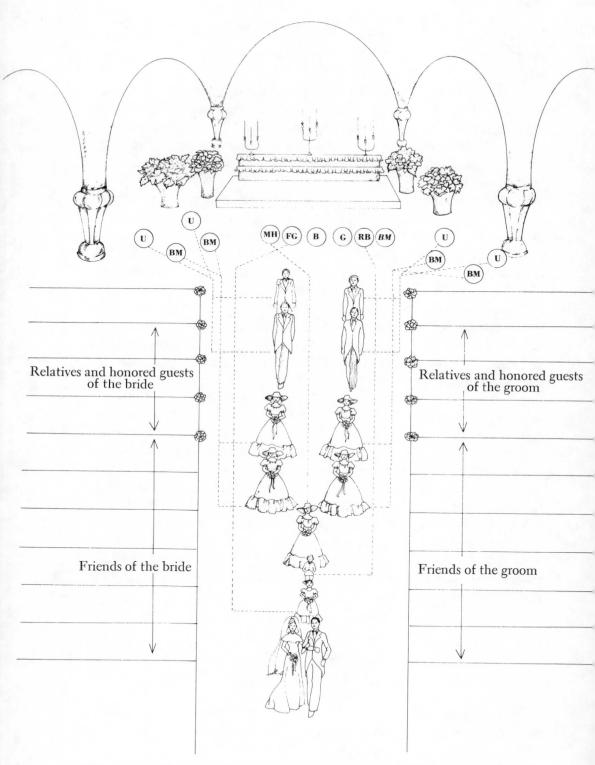

The recessional: B, Bride; G, Groom; BM, Best Man; FG, Flower Girl; RB, Ring Bearer; BM, Bridesmaid; U, Usher

As people arrive, they are greeted by the ushers, who inquire whether they will be sitting on the bride's side (usually the left) or the groom's side (usually the right). If several women arrive together, they should all be escorted by ushers, if possible, with the first usher offering his arm to the oldest woman present. The other women follow. Male escorts follow behind the usher. As the pews are filled, the ushers should remove the pew ribbons, if present.

Relatives and other honored guests are seated in reserved pews just behind the parents. Often these pews are ribboned off, and special cards may be sent to the guests who will be seated there. To avoid possible confusion or embarrassment, the head usher should be given a list of the guests to be seated within the ribbons. During the last few minutes before the wedding begins, brothers and sisters of the bride and groom are seated behind their parents' pews. Five minutes before the ceremony, the groom's parents are seated in the first pew on their side. When your mother arrives, the head usher goes to the back of the church to alert the groom that the wedding is about to begin. Then he returns to seat your mother, who is always the last person seated. If aisle ribbons have been used, they are removed at this time. The white carpet, if there is any, is rolled down the aisle. Tomorrow the wedding will begin at this point; tonight the rehearsal will end and the wedding party, parents, and families head for the rehearsal dinner, hosted by the groom's parents. The party is festive and gay, but it shouldn't last very late, as everyone will want to be in good shape for the wedding. Enjoy the rehearsal and the party and then go home and get a good night's sleep, for tomorrow will be—your wedding day!

Your Wedding Day

Finally, the big day has arrived. However excited you are, it is still a day to take with leisure, to enjoy, and to cherish for all its magic moments.

If you have planned and organized carefully, there should be no last-minute worries to mar this special day. Your hair and make-up should be perfect, your nails beautifully manicured.

Your dress is ready. After the final fitting, bring the dress to your house. Hang it on a high door, so the weight of the fabric will smooth out the wrinkles. Detach the train and hang it flat or place it on a large bed where it will be undisturbed. If a touch-up is necessary, steam-press the dress on the wrong side. Should true disaster strike, in the form of a lipstick or other kind of stain or a tear in the lace, call the shop or store where you bought the dress. They can best recommend how to repair the damage.

Have a leisurely breakfast with your family before you start to dress. Now is the time to let your hospitality committee and your mother assume their responsibilities. The hospitality committee will function at the reception, and your mother will be sure everything is coming together to make your wedding day as smooth and beautiful as possible. She will oversee the photographer, caterer, and florist.

As the hour of the wedding approaches, be sure to allow yourself enough time to prepare so the wedding can begin promptly on time. Many churches book several weddings on one day and the minister's time is valuable, so it is a courtesy to everyone involved to make sure everything follows the time schedule that has been set up.

The best man will ride herd on the groom and the groomsmen, so you need not worry about that.

Your bridesmaids have been told by you to report either to the church or to your home, and rides have been arranged to get them where they are supposed to be (this is a task for which cousins and brothers come in handy). If there is a dressing room at the church, that is the best place for all of you to dress.

When you leave for the church, be sure to take your dress and its accessories, a white lace-edged handkerchief, extra hose, facial tissue or white handkerchiefs for your bridesmaids and the mothers, a comb, make-up for touch-ups, and cologne. Tuck the beauty aids in a beaded or cloth evening purse. Be sure to spread a sheet over the car seat and floor for the dress. You should arrive at the church an hour in advance if you plan to dress there, even earlier if your bridal portrait will be taken there. If possible, bring a thermos of lemonade or some other refreshing drink and small sandwiches. In all the excitement of the day, some people may not have eaten enough, so the last-minute snack may forestall faintness during the ceremony.

As soon as you and your bridesmaids are dressed, the florist will show you how to carry your flowers. Pass out the handkerchiefs to your bridesmaids and mothers, but take a minute to remind everyone that this is a happy and joyous occasion and there is really no need for tears.

As you are making last-minute preparations, the guests will be arriving and the prelude music will be playing. Five minutes before the ceremony is due to begin, the mother and father of the groom are seated. About one or two minutes before, your mother is escorted to her seat, and the bridesmaids are lining up at the back of the church.

In most churches, when the processional begins, the guests stand. They may stand throughout the ceremony, kneel, or sit, according to the signals given by the minister. As your bridesmaids start down the aisle, take your father's arm and stand in position. When the music changes, take a deep breath and step forward on your left foot to walk down the aisle to meet your waiting groom.

AFTER THE CEREMONY

As soon as you reach the back of the church, if wedding pictures will be taken, you and the wedding party should walk around to the door where the groom entered with the minister and wait there until all the guests have left the church. Meet at the altar for portraits of the wedding party. The photographer should have been told that you want these pictures taken quickly so you do not keep your guests waiting too long at the reception. You may also have to meet with the minister to sign and witness the marriage certificate.

THE RECEIVING LINE

If the receiving line is formed at the back of the church, the pictures are taken immediately afterward. If the reception is somewhere other than the church, immediately after the pictures are taken the wedding party goes in prearranged transportation to the reception, where the receiving line is usually formed. After all the guests have gone through the receiving line, pictures may be taken of it. Guests always enjoy watching this, and it is more tactful to take these pictures after the receiving line than to keep guests waiting outside. Drinks should be served to guests as they walk away from the receiving line; a member of the hospitality committee can stand nearby and direct them to the refreshment table or bar.

On pages 131–32 are two variations of the receiving line. The bride's mother, as official hostess, should always be the first person in the line. If the bride has no mother, an aunt or grandmother can be asked to serve as hostess. Neither father has to stand in line; each may circulate among the guests if he prefers. The bridesmaids are also optional to the receiving line. If they do stand in the line, they should position themselves after the maid or matron of honor. The best man does not usually stand in the receiving line.

If there will be a long delay between the time the ceremony is over and when the wedding party is able to arrive at the reception, have members of the hospitality committee speed to the reception site and

The Receiving Line: Left to Right: Mother of the Bride, Father of the Groom, Mother of the Groom, Father of the Bride, Bride, Groom, Maid or Matron of Honor, Bridesmaid, Bridesmaid

offer drinks to waiting guests, who then go through the receiving line when you do arrive.

THE BRIDE'S TABLE

When there is a sit-down wedding breakfast, luncheon, or supper, seating at the bride's table is arranged in this way:

As a rule, only the bridal party is seated at the bride's table, although husbands and wives of attendants may be invited to sit at it, too, if there is room. The bride and groom sit next to each other—you on his right. Even if guests serve themselves at a buffet table, the bride's table is served by waiters or a serving committee. Place cards are necessary only on the bride's table and parents' table, but they may be used on all tables. The wedding cake may be centered on your table in front of the bride and groom, or it may be on a separate table just for that purpose.

(131)

The Receiving Line: Left to Right: Mother of the Bride, Mother of the Groom, Bride, Groom, Maid or Matron of Honor, Bridesmaid, Bridesmaid, Father of the Groom, Father of the Bride

The Bride's Table: Left to Right: Bridesmaid, Usher, Bridesmaid, Best Man, Bride, Groom, Maid or Matron of Honor, Usher, Bridesmaid, Usher

At a stand-up reception it is thoughtful to have a few tables at the sides and in the corners for older people.

Your reception is a celebration in your honor, a lovely party. Although you are the guests of honor, you are, in a sense, the host and hostess, and it is up to you and your new husband to mingle with the guests and make them feel at home. Intimate family friends and relatives who have not already been invited are encouraged to drop by the postreception open house at your parents' home.

Enjoy yourself—this is one party at which you should and will, of course, have the time of your life.

THE PARENTS' TABLE

The parents of the bride and groom and other members of the intimate family, and the minister and his wife, are seated at a separate table nearby. Your father sits at the head of the table with the groom's mother to his right. Your mother sits at the foot of the table with the groom's father at her right.

TOASTS AT THE RECEPTION

The best man offers the toasts during the reception; he proposes the first toast to you and your groom as soon as the beverages are served.

The toast may be very brief. "To Jackie and Rusty, may they always be as happy as they are today." Everyone rises to drink to your happiness while you and the groom remain seated and smile in acknowledgment and say thank you to those around you. The next toast is usually made by the groom, who thanks the best man and then toasts your parents: "To my mother-in-law and my father-in-law, two wonderful people without whom this wedding could not have been possible." Next the groom's father says something like, "To our beautiful daughter-in-law, Jackie, who doesn't need to be told how happy we are to have her in our family." Then the bride's father toasts, "To our daughter and son-in-law, may God bless you always." Others may then propose toasts if they wish, but someone, probably the best man, should be sure the toasting doesn't get out of hand. After the toasts, the best man reads aloud any telegrams that have arrived wishing you and your groom happiness.

THE WEDDING CAKE

The cutting of the wedding cake is always a highlight of the reception. When it is time to cut it, you and the groom and all the gentlemen at the table stand. The guests have been signaled by a fanfare or by the clinking of a glass by the best man. Usually a silver cake knife with a beribboned handle is used. The groom places his hand over your hand on the knife handle, and together, you cut the first slice, which is shared by you as a symbol of your willingness to share each others lives.

After the first ceremonial piece is cut, someone usually steps in to complete the cutting.

DANCING

When there is dancing at a reception, by tradition the bride and groom dance the first dance alone for a minute or two. Then your father cuts in on the groom to dance with you, and the groom dances with your mother. Fourth, the groom's parents come to the floor, and the groom's father dances with you. Fifth, your father cuts in on the groom and dances with his wife. Sixth, the groom then dances with his mother. Seventh, your parents exchange dances with the groom's parents. Eighth, the best man dances with you. Ninth, the groom dances with the maid of honor. Finally the wedding party—bridesmaids and ushers—join on the dance floor. When the whole wedding party is on the dance floor, the other guests are invited to dance.

THE GUEST BOOK TABLE

An elegant and traditional touch for the reception is the guest book table. This can be any small table decorated with a cloth and greenery or bows, with one or two high-backed chairs for the guest book attend-

ants. The attendants should offer the pen (a quill pen is a nice touch) and book to each guest.

TOSSING YOUR BOUQUET AND GARTER

Before you leave the reception to change into your going-away outfit, let your bridesmaids know so they can gather to catch the bouquet. You may also throw your garter at this time if you wish. Your mother or maid of honor may help you change into street clothes.

When you and your husband are ready to leave, take a few minutes to say good-by to your parents and attendants; thank everyone for making your day so special. Rose petals, confetti, or rice are tossed at you by guests as you leave. The departure of the bride and groom generally signals the end of the reception.

21
Calling It Off

Although every couple to some extent has doubts and last-minute jitters, most go through with the wedding. Knowing that a mild case of nerves is perfectly normal, however, shouldn't stop either person from calling off the wedding if there are serious doubts.

A broken engagement is painful for everyone involved, but it is better than an unhappy marriage. If the engagement has not been formally announced, you can simply pass the word to a few close friends who will tell other people. A detailed explanation—or indeed, any explanation—is not required, and tactful friends will not press for one. You need only say that you have broken up. Why you have made such a decision is strictly your own business.

If the engagement has been formally announced in the papers, a brief announcement to the effect that it is now broken is in order. It usually reads:

> Mr. and Mrs. Bruce Long Jones announce that the engagement of their daughter Jane Ann and Mr. George James Adams has been ended by mutual consent.

If the wedding invitations have been sent, a printed announcement must be prepared and mailed as soon as possible, if there is time before the wedding. (If there is not time, the word must be passed quickly by telegram and telephone.) Any announcement could be worded as follows:

Mr. and Mrs. Bruce Long Jones
announce that the marriage of their daughter
Jane Ann
to
Mr. George James Adams
will not take place

A telegram could be worded: "The marriage of our daughter Jane Ann to Mr. George James Adams will not take place. Mr. and Mrs. Bruce Long Jones."

As soon as the wedding is called off, notify all persons involved in supplying items, such as the baker, the florist, and the photographer; also notify the clergyman and others involved.

Occasionally these days, there is cause to postpone a wedding because of a family emergency such as illness or death. Again, the wedding guests are notified, as are all suppliers, as soon as possible. Such an announcement to prospective wedding guests usually includes an explanation. If there is time, formal announcements may be printed; otherwise, notes are written in the following format:

Mr. and Mrs. Marshall Mark Stark
regret that they are obliged to recall
the invitations to the marriage of their daughter
Andrea Sue to Mr. John Park Stone
owing to the death of Mr. Stone's father
Mr. Harold Travers Stone

To the above can be added the following lines:

The ceremony will be held privately
in the presence of the immediate family

If invitations to a reception must be recalled:

Mr. and Mrs. Marshall Mark Stark
regret that owing to a death in the family
they are obliged to recall the invitations
to the marriage reception of their daughter
on Friday, the twenty-fourth of April.
The marriage ceremony will take place
as originally planned.

22

Now That You're Married

USING YOUR NEW NAME

Many women use their new married names in one form or another after
they are married. There are a few simple guidelines that will help you
in using your new name. You were Jacqueline Marie Young before
your marriage. You married John Anthony Gray. Mrs. John Anthony
Gray becomes your formal married name, if you choose to use it. It is
the name you have engraved on informal fold-over note cards and your
calling card. The choice of full names versus initials is a personal one.

There is a growing trend among young women to keep their own
names after marriage either in business or sometimes in all facets of
their lives. If this is your choice, the first step is to check the legal requirements of the state you reside in. For example, in some states, a
bride must petition to keep her name; in other states, she need only
inform the county clerk or registrar. If you have decided to keep your
own name, you will probably want to tell friends informally and to include this fact in newspaper announcements of your wedding. If you
use your own name all the time, you have the option of having it
printed on any stationery you may buy rather than using your formal
married name.

ABOUT MONOGRAMS

The use of a monogram on luggage, linens, and clothes is an old bridal tradition that many brides still follow today. Such monograms use the first initial of your first name, the initial of your maiden name, and the first initial of your husband's surname. On silver and as a second choice for linens, the initial of your husband's surname is preferred.

SIGNING LETTERS

If you don't change your name, you won't have to worry about your new signature. Should you elect to call yourself Mrs. John Anthony Gray, you still never sign anything "Mrs. John Anthony Gray." Use your name, Jacqueline Gray, in whatever form you choose, on legal papers, checks, and letters. On business correspondence relating to your household, you may sign "Mrs. John Anthony Gray" in parentheses under or to the left of your signature or typed name. "Mrs. Jacqueline Young (your maiden name) Gray" is never correct.

IN HOTELS, CLUBS, CHURCHES, AND STORES

In these places, you may use your married name with the "Mrs." In such cases, the "Mrs." preceding your name is important for identification purposes.

INTRODUCING EACH OTHER

Husbands and wives do not refer to each other during introductions as "Mr. Gray" or "Mrs. Gray." Nor should a man refer to his wife as "the missus," "the wife," or "the better half." Simply say, "May I introduce my husband," or "This is my wife." If the woman has kept her own name, the man may want to repeat it when introducing her to a stranger.

A PARTY TO THANK EVERYONE

Although it is not required, one of the loveliest gestures you can make is to invite everyone who helped to make your wedding successful to be the first guests in your new home. Be sure to include everyone who had a shower or entertained for you. This is a time to show off your honeymoon pictures and wedding gifts. You will be loved for this extra touch of thoughtfulness.

The Bride's Organizer

OUR ENGAGEMENT ANNOUNCEMENT

Our Wedding Traditions

The weather on our wedding day was ⸺

⸺

Wedding ring traditions ⸺

⸺

Something old ⸺
Something new ⸺
Something borrowed ⸺
Something blue ⸺
And a lucky sixpence in your shoe! ⸺

⸺

My bouquet was caught by ⸺
My garter was caught by ⸺
I was given away by ⸺
Showers were given by ⸺
　　　　　　on ⸺
　　　　　　at ⸺
　　　　　　by ⸺
　　　　　　on ⸺
　　　　　　at ⸺
The cake surprise went to ⸺
The bachelor party took place on ⸺
　　　　　　at ⸺
Other traditions ⸺

⸺

⸺

⸺

⸺

⸺

⸺

⸺

(147)

Cost Estimates for Wedding and Reception Services

	First Bid	Second Bid	Actual Cost
RECEPTION SITE			
Church basement	$_____	$_____	$_____
Banquet room of hotel or restaurant	$_____	$_____	$_____
Private club	$_____	$_____	$_____
Other	$_____	$_____	$_____
Total	$_____	$_____	$_____
PRINTING			
Invitations	$_____	$_____	$_____
Reception cards	$_____	$_____	$_____
Announcements	$_____	$_____	$_____
At-home cards	$_____	$_____	$_____
Informals	$_____	$_____	$_____
Thank-you cards	$_____	$_____	$_____
Reception napkins	$_____	$_____	$_____
Matches	$_____	$_____	$_____
Cake boxes	$_____	$_____	$_____
Extras	$_____	$_____	$_____
Total	$_____	$_____	$_____
FLOWERS			
Wedding			
Church, home, hotel, etc.	$_____	$_____	$_____
Bouquets	$_____	$_____	$_____
Corsages	$_____	$_____	$_____
Boutonnieres	$_____	$_____	$_____
Total	$_____	$_____	$_____
Reception			
Receiving line	$_____	$_____	$_____
Buffet centerpieces	$_____	$_____	$_____
Table decorations	$_____	$_____	$_____
Cake table	$_____	$_____	$_____
Guest book table	$_____	$_____	$_____
Total	$_____	$_____	$_____

Cost Estimates for Wedding and Reception Services

	First Bid	Second Bid	Actual Cost
WEDDING ATTIRE			
Wedding gown	$_____	$_____	$_____
Veil	$_____	$_____	$_____
Accessories	$_____	$_____	$_____
Trousseau	$_____	$_____	$_____
Total	$_____	$_____	$_____
PHOTOGRAPHY			
Engagement portrait	$_____	$_____	$_____
Wedding portrait	$_____	$_____	$_____
Candids	$_____	$_____	$_____
Duplicate prints for groom's parents, attendants, etc.	$_____	$_____	$_____
Total	$_____	$_____	$_____
MUSIC			
Wedding	$_____	$_____	$_____
Reception	$_____	$_____	$_____
Rehearsal	$_____	$_____	$_____
Rehearsal dinner	$_____	$_____	$_____
Total	$_____	$_____	$_____
FOOD, BEVERAGES, AND SERVICE			
Bridal Luncheon	$_____	$_____	$_____
Rehearsal Dinner	$_____	$_____	$_____
Reception			
Food	$_____	$_____	$_____
Liquor	$_____	$_____	$_____
Nonalcoholic beverages	$_____	$_____	$_____
Wedding cake	$_____	$_____	$_____
Service (waiters, bartenders, etc.)	$_____	$_____	$_____
Total	$_____	$_____	$_____

Cost Estimates for Wedding and
Reception Services

DONATIONS

Church . . . . $_____

Minister . . . . $_____

Sexton . . . . $_____

Organist . . . . $_____ $_____ $_____

Janitors at church . . . . $_____

Wedding consultant at church . . . . $_____

Police officer in charge of traffic and
 parking in front of church . . . . $_____

              Total $_____

GIFTS

Attendants . . . . $_____ $_____ $_____

Groom . . . . $_____ $_____ $_____

Wedding ring for groom . . . . $_____ $_____ $_____

     Total $_____ $_____ $_____

TRANSPORTATION . . . . $_____ $_____ $_____

MISCELLANEOUS

Table favors . . . . $_____ $_____ $_____

Candles . . . . $_____ $_____ $_____

Hotel accommodations . . . . $_____ $_____ $_____

Prerehearsal party . . . . $_____ $_____ $_____

Mother's gown and accessories . . . . $_____ $_____ $_____

Father's outfit and accessories . . . . . $_____ $_____ $_____

Others . . . . $_____ $_____ $_____

      Total $_____ $_____ $_____

TOTAL WEDDING COST . . . . . $_____ $_____ $_____

Important Names, Addresses, and Appointments

Person in charge of wedding site ———— Phone ————
Address ———————————— Appt. ————

Clergy or ceremony official ———— Phone ————
Address ———————————— Appt. ————

Church wedding consultant ———— Phone ————
Address ———————————— Appt. ————

Organist ———————————— Phone ————
Address ———————————— Appt. ————

Soloist ———————————— Phone ————
Address ———————————— Appt. ————

Printer/stationer ———————— Phone ————
Address ———————————— Appt. ————

Florist ———————————— Phone ————
Address ———————————— Appt. ————

Baker ———————————— Phone ————
Address ———————————— Appt. ————

Photographer ———————— Phone ————
Address ———————————— Appt. ————

Travel agent ———————— Phone ————
Address ———————————— Appt. ————

Doctor ———————————— Phone ————
Address ———————————— Appt. ————

Jeweler ———————————— Phone ————
Address ———————————— Appt. ————

Bridal consultant ———— Store ———— Phone ————
Address ———————————— Appt. ————

Bridal consultant ———— Store ———— Phone ————
Address ———————————— Appt. ————

Important Names, Addresses, and Appointments

Bridal consultant ——————— Store ——— Phone ———

Address ————————————— Appt. ———

Bridal consultant ——————— Store ——— Phone ———

Address ————————————— Appt. ———

Seamstress for bride's, attendants', and

    flower girl's gowns ———————— Phone ———

Address ————————————— Appt. ———

Hairdresser ———————————— Phone ———

Address ————————————— Appt. ———

Limousine service ———————— Phone ———

Address ————————————— Appt. ———

Manager of hotel where out-of-town

    guests will stay ————————— Phone ———

Address ————————————— Appt. ———

Person in charge of reception site ——— Phone ———

Address ————————————— Appt. ———

Caterer —————————————— Phone ———

Address ————————————— Appt. ———

Musicians for reception ——————— Phone ———

Address ————————————— Appt. ———

Others ——————————————— Phone ———

Address ————————————— Appt. ———

Others ——————————————— Phone ———

Address ————————————— Appt. ———

Others ——————————————— Phone ———

Address ————————————— Appt. ———

Others ——————————————— Phone ———

Address ————————————— Appt. ———

Transportation Checklist

Drivers to church and to reception

Bride to church with father (or father and mother):
Driver ——————————————————— Phone ——————
Time to be at house ————————————————————

Bridesmaids to church and return for reception:
Driver ————————————— Phone ——————— Time ————
Bridesmaid's address ————————————————— Phone ————
Driver ————————————— Phone ——————— Time ————
Bridesmaid's address ————————————————— Phone ————
Driver ————————————— Phone ——————— Time ————
Bridesmaid's address ————————————————— Phone ————
Driver ————————————— Phone ——————— Time ————
Bridesmaid's address ————————————————— Phone ————
Driver ————————————— Phone ——————— Time ————
Bridesmaid's address ————————————————— Phone ————

Bride's mother, unless she rides with bride or bridesmaids:
Driver ————————————— Phone ——————— Time ————
Bride's parents' address ————————————— Phone ————
Driver ————————————— Phone ——————— Time ————

Bride's grandparents:
Driver ————————————— Phone ——————— Time ————

Groom's parents:
Driver ————————————— Phone ——————— Time ————
Address ————————————————————————————

Groom's grandparents' address ——————————————————
    Phone ————————————————————————————
Driver ————————————— Phone ——————— Time ————

Bride and groom to reception:
    Phone ————————————————————————————
Driver ————————————————————— Phone ————

Transportation Checklist for Out-of-Town Guests

ARRIVING

Date	Person to be met	Place	Time	Address to be taken to	Person responsible

(154)

Transportation Checklist for Out-of-Town Guests

DEPARTING

Date	Person to be met	Place	Time	Address to be taken to	Person responsible

(155)

Sample Form for Wedding Announcement

To: Society Editor   For Release: _____

Full name of bride _____
Full name of bride's parents _____
Address _____ Phone _____
Bride's schools _____ When? _____
Bride's affiliations _____
Full name of bridegroom _____
Full name of bridegroom's parents _____
Address _____ Phone _____
Bridegroom's schools _____ When? _____
Bridegroom's affiliations _____
Wedding date and time _____
Wedding place _____
Reception place _____
Honeymoon _____
Future home _____
Bride's honor attendants _____ Best Man _____
_____ Ushers _____
Her other attendants _____ _____
_____ _____
_____
_____ Clergyman _____
Giving bride in marriage _____
Bride's gown _____
_____
Veil _____ Bouquet _____
Attendants' costumes _____
_____
_____ Flowers _____
Decorations at church _____
Decorations at reception _____
Bride's mother's costume _____
Bridegroom's mother's costume _____
Going-away costume _____
_____
Out-of-town guests were from _____
_____
_____

Our Wedding Party

Maid (or Matron) of Honor _____ Phone _____
Address _____
Dress size _____ Bust _____ Waist _____ Hips _____
Sleeve (shoulder to wrist) _____ Neck _____ Head _____
Length (waist to floor) _____ Glove size _____ Shoe size _____

Bridesmaid _____ Phone _____
Address _____
Dress size _____ Bust _____ Waist _____ Hips _____
Sleeve (shoulder to wrist) _____ Neck _____ Head _____
Length (waist to floor) _____ Glove size _____ Shoe size _____

Bridesmaid _____ Phone _____
Address _____
Dress size _____ Bust _____ Waist _____ Hips _____
Sleeve (shoulder to wrist) _____ Neck _____ Head _____
Length (waist to floor) _____ Glove size _____ Shoe size _____

Bridesmaid _____ Phone _____
Address _____
Dress size _____ Bust _____ Waist _____ Hips _____
Sleeve (shoulder to wrist) _____ Neck _____ Head _____
Length (waist to floor) _____ Glove size _____ Shoe size _____

Bridesmaid _____ Phone _____
Address _____
Dress size _____ Bust _____ Waist _____ Hips _____
Sleeve (shoulder to wrist) _____ Neck _____ Head _____
Length (waist to floor) _____ Glove size _____ Shoe size _____

Bridesmaid _____ Phone _____
Address _____
Dress size _____ Bust _____ Waist _____ Hips _____
Sleeve (shoulder to wrist) _____ Neck _____ Head _____
Length (waist to floor) _____ Glove size _____ Shoe size _____

Our Wedding Party

Bridesmaid ———————————————————— Phone ————

Address ——————————————————————————————

Dress size ———— Bust ———— Waist ———— Hips ————

Sleeve (shoulder to wrist) ———— Neck ———— Head ————

Length (waist to floor) ———— Glove size ———— Shoe size ————

Bridesmaid ———————————————————— Phone ————

Address ——————————————————————————————

Dress size ———— Bust ———— Waist ———— Hips ————

Sleeve (shoulder to wrist) ———— Neck ———— Head ————

Length (waist to floor) ———— Glove size ———— Shoe size ————

Bridesmaid ———————————————————— Phone ————

Address ——————————————————————————————

Dress size ———— Bust ———— Waist ———— Hips ————

Sleeve (shoulder to wrist) ———— Neck ———— Head ————

Length (waist to floor) ———— Glove size ———— Shoe size ————

Best Man ———————————————————— Phone ————

Address ——————————————————————————————

Waist ———— Inseam ———— Shoe size ————

Glove size ———— Jacket size ———— Shirt size ————

Usher ———————————————————— Phone ————

Address ——————————————————————————————

Waist ———— Inseam ———— Shoe size ————

Glove size ———— Jacket size ———— Shirt size ————

Usher ———————————————————— Phone ————

Address ——————————————————————————————

Waist ———— Inseam ———— Shoe size ————

Glove size ———— Jacket size ———— Shirt size ————

Usher ———————————————————— Phone ————

Address ——————————————————————————————

Waist ———— Inseam ———— Shoe size ————

Glove size ———— Jacket size ———— Shirt size ————

Our Wedding Party

Usher ——————————————————————— Phone ————
Address ———————————————————————————
Waist ————— Inseam ————— Shoe size —————
Glove size ————— Jacket size ————— Shirt size —————

Usher ——————————————————————— Phone ————
Address ———————————————————————————
Waist ————— Inseam ————— Shoe size —————
Glove size ————— Jacket size ————— Shirt size —————

Usher ——————————————————————— Phone ————
Address ———————————————————————————
Waist ————— Inseam ————— Shoe size —————
Glove size ————— Jacket size ————— Shirt size —————

Usher ——————————————————————— Phone ————
Address ———————————————————————————
Waist ————— Inseam ————— Shoe size —————
Glove size ————— Jacket size ————— Shirt size —————

Usher ——————————————————————— Phone ————
Address ———————————————————————————
Waist ————— Inseam ————— Shoe size —————
Glove size ————— Jacket size ————— Shirt size —————

Usher ——————————————————————— Phone ————
Address ———————————————————————————
Waist ————— Inseam ————— Shoe size —————
Glove size ————— Jacket size ————— Shirt size —————

Usher ——————————————————————— Phone ————
Address ———————————————————————————
Waist ————— Inseam ————— Shoe size —————
Glove size ————— Jacket size ————— Shirt size —————

Usher ——————————————————————— Phone ————
Address ———————————————————————————
Waist ————— Inseam ————— Shoe size —————
Glove size ————— Jacket size ————— Shirt size —————

Our Wedding Party

Flower girl _____ Phone _____

Address _____

Dress size _____ Bust _____ Waist _____ Hips _____

Sleeve (shoulder to wrist) _____ Neck _____ Head _____

Length (waist to floor) _____ Glove size _____ Shoe size _____

Ring bearer _____ Phone _____

Address _____

Waist _____ Inseam _____ Shoe size _____

Glove size _____ Jacket size _____ Shirt size _____

Special attendant _____ Phone _____

Address _____

Special attendant _____ Phone _____

Address _____

Special attendant _____ Phone _____

Address _____

Special attendant _____ Phone _____

Address _____

Overall supervisor _____ Phone _____

Address _____

Groom's parents _____ Phone _____

Address _____

_____ Phone _____

Address _____

Our Wedding Ceremony Music

(Copies to be given to all musicians and soloists)

Prelude selections (to begin _____ minutes before the ceremony):

_____

_____

_____

_____

_____

_____

First solo (to be sung _____ minutes before the ceremony):

_____

Second solo (to be sung _____ minutes before the ceremony):

_____

Processional (to be played after bride's mother is seated):

_____

Music to be played during ceremony (optional):

_____

_____

Recessional _____

_____

_____

Name of soloist _____ Phone _____

Address _____ Fee _____

Name of musician _____ Phone _____

Address _____ Fee _____

Florist's Information Sheet

(Copy to be given to florist)

Name of bride _____ Phone _____

Address _____

Ceremony date _____ Time _____ Location _____

_____

Reception time _____ Location _____

_____

Color and type of wedding dress _____

Color, size, and type of bridal bouquet _____

_____ Ribbon color _____ Cost _____

Color and type of corsage for bride's going-away costume _____

_____ Cost _____

Bride's mother _____

    Color of dress _____ Type of corsage _____ Cost _____

    Corsage to be sent to _____ Date _____ Time _____

Groom's mother _____

    Color of dress _____ Type of corsage _____ Cost _____

    Corsage to be sent to _____ Date _____ Time _____

Bride's grandmother(s) _____ _____

    Type of corsage _____ Cost _____

    Corsage to be sent to _____ Date _____ Time _____

    _____ Date _____ Time _____

Groom's grandmother(s) _____ _____

    Type of corsage _____ Cost _____

    Corsage to be sent to _____ Date _____ Time _____

    _____ Date _____ Time _____

Material sample of bridesmaids' dresses

Material sample of flower girl's dress

Color, size, and type of attendants' bouquets _____

_____ Ribbon color _____ Cost _____

Style and type of flowers for floral headdresses, if these are being used

_____ Cost _____

(162)

Amount and type of petals or flowers for flower girl's basket _____
_____ Cost _____
Bridal bouquet and all attendants' flowers to be delivered to _____
_____
Date _____ Time _____
Number and type of boutonnieres desired for the groom, best man,
ushers, and fathers _____ Cost _____
Boutonnieres to be delivered to _____
Date _____ Time _____
Names and addresses of relatives, friends, organist, soloist, reception
servers, and others who are to be sent corsages; color and type of cor-
sages to be sent; date and time to be sent: Cost _____

1. _____   2. _____
   _____   _____
   _____   _____
   _____   _____

Date _____ Time _____   Date _____ Time _____
3. _____   4. _____
   _____   _____
   _____   _____
   _____   _____

Date _____ Time _____   Date _____ Time _____

Church Decorations

Cushion to be supplied for ring bearer: Yes _____ No _____ Cost_____
Aisle carpet: Yes _____ No _____ Cost _____
Type and color of flowers to be used in church decorations _____
_____
_____ Cost _____
Number of aisles to be decorated _____
Type and color of flowers to be used in aisle decorations _____
_____ Cost _____
Aisle ribbons to be used: Yes _____ No _____ Cost _____
All church flowers and decorations to be delivered to _____
_____ Date _____ Time_____
Person to contact at church for additional information _____
_____ Phone_____

(163)

Reception Decorations

Type and color of flowers to be used for the reception decorations:
Receiving line background ⎯⎯⎯⎯⎯⎯⎯⎯⎯⎯⎯⎯⎯⎯⎯⎯⎯⎯⎯⎯⎯⎯
⎯⎯⎯⎯⎯⎯⎯⎯⎯⎯⎯⎯⎯⎯⎯⎯⎯⎯⎯⎯⎯⎯ Cost ⎯⎯⎯⎯

Centerpieces:
  Bride's table ⎯⎯⎯⎯⎯⎯⎯⎯⎯⎯⎯⎯ Cost ⎯⎯⎯⎯
  Parents' table ⎯⎯⎯⎯⎯⎯⎯⎯⎯⎯⎯ Cost ⎯⎯⎯⎯
  Buffet tables: How many ⎯⎯⎯⎯⎯⎯⎯⎯⎯⎯⎯⎯⎯⎯⎯⎯
              Type and color ⎯⎯⎯⎯⎯⎯⎯⎯ Cost ⎯⎯⎯⎯
  Guests' tables: How many ⎯⎯⎯⎯⎯⎯⎯⎯⎯⎯⎯⎯⎯⎯⎯⎯
              Type and color ⎯⎯⎯⎯⎯⎯⎯⎯ Cost ⎯⎯⎯⎯
  Guest book table ⎯⎯⎯⎯⎯⎯⎯⎯⎯⎯⎯ Cost ⎯⎯⎯⎯
  Wedding cake table ⎯⎯⎯⎯⎯⎯⎯⎯⎯⎯ Cost ⎯⎯⎯⎯
White satin ribbons and flowers secured on wedding knife: Yes ⎯⎯⎯⎯
No ⎯⎯⎯⎯ Cost ⎯⎯⎯⎯
Small flowers with white satin ribbons tied to stems of champagne toast
  glasses: Yes ⎯⎯⎯⎯ No ⎯⎯⎯⎯ Cost ⎯⎯⎯⎯
Greens and fresh red rose petals to surround wedding cake: Yes⎯⎯⎯⎯
No ⎯⎯⎯⎯ Cost ⎯⎯⎯⎯
All reception flowers and bride's going-away corsage to be delivered to
⎯⎯⎯⎯⎯⎯⎯⎯⎯⎯⎯⎯⎯⎯⎯⎯ Date ⎯⎯⎯⎯⎯ Time⎯⎯⎯⎯
Person to contact at reception site for additional information ⎯⎯⎯⎯
⎯⎯⎯⎯⎯⎯⎯⎯⎯⎯⎯⎯⎯⎯⎯⎯⎯⎯⎯⎯ Phone ⎯⎯⎯⎯

Bridal Luncheon Decorations

Type and color of flowers ⎯⎯⎯⎯⎯⎯⎯⎯⎯⎯⎯⎯⎯⎯⎯⎯⎯⎯
⎯⎯⎯⎯⎯⎯⎯⎯⎯⎯⎯⎯⎯⎯⎯⎯⎯⎯⎯⎯ Cost ⎯⎯⎯⎯
Flowers to be delivered to ⎯⎯⎯⎯⎯⎯⎯⎯⎯⎯⎯⎯⎯⎯⎯⎯⎯⎯
  Date ⎯⎯⎯⎯⎯⎯⎯⎯⎯ Time ⎯⎯⎯⎯⎯⎯⎯⎯

Rehearsal Dinner Decorations

Type and color of flowers ⎯⎯⎯⎯⎯⎯⎯⎯⎯⎯⎯⎯⎯⎯⎯⎯⎯⎯
⎯⎯⎯⎯⎯⎯⎯⎯⎯⎯⎯⎯⎯⎯⎯⎯⎯⎯⎯⎯ Cost ⎯⎯⎯⎯
Number of centerpieces ⎯⎯⎯⎯⎯⎯⎯⎯⎯⎯⎯ Cost ⎯⎯⎯⎯
Flowers to be delivered to ⎯⎯⎯⎯⎯⎯⎯⎯⎯⎯⎯⎯⎯⎯⎯⎯⎯⎯
  Date ⎯⎯⎯⎯⎯⎯⎯⎯⎯ Time ⎯⎯⎯⎯⎯⎯⎯⎯

Flowers for After the Wedding

Type and color of thank-you flowers for mothers, friends, and relatives
who helped with wedding _____

_____ Cost _____

Where and when to deliver:

1. _____

_____

_____

Date _____

2. _____

_____

_____

Date _____

3. _____

_____

_____

Date _____

4. _____

_____

_____

Date _____

Musical Organization for the Reception

(Copy to be given to musicians)

Name of bride ―――――――――――――― Phone ――――

Address ――――――――――――――――――――――――――

Reception date ―――――――――――――― Time ――――――

Location ―――――――――――――――――――――――――――

Time of arrival for musicians ―――――――――― Cost ――――

Music to begin as first guests arrive (light, joyous music) ――――

――――――――――――――――――――――――――――――――

Music to be played as wedding party arrives ――――――――――

――――――――――――――――――――――――――――――――

Music to be played as guests go through receiving line (old standards are "When I Fall in Love," "It Had to Be You," "I'll Be Loving You Always," "Autumn Leaves") ――――――――――――――――――

――――――――――――――――――――――――――――――――

――――――――――――――――――――――――――――――――

Music to be played as wedding party sits down to eat (your favorite songs) ―――――――――――――――――――――――――――

――――――――――――――――――――――――――――――――

Music to be played for the first dance
1. Bride and groom ("The Girl That I Marry") ――――――――

――――――――――――――――――――――――――――――――

2. Father and bride ("Thank Heaven for Little Girls") ――――

――――――――――――――――――――――――――――――――

3. Groom with mother of bride ("I Want a Girl Just Like the Girl That Married Dear Old Dad") ―――――――――――――――
4. Groom's Father with Bride ("True Love") ――――――――――
5. Bride's Father with Bride's Mother ("When I Fall in Love") ――

――――――――――――――――――――――――――――――――

Other music to be played ――――――――――――――――――

――――――――――――――――――――――――――――――――

――――――――――――――――――――――――――――――――

Music to be played as fanfares (watch ――――――― for signals)
· During cake-cutting ――――――――――――――――――――
As bride tosses her bouquet ――――――――――――――――
As groom throws bride's garter ――――――――――――――
As bride and groom leave the reception ―――――――――――

(166)

Alcoholic Beverages for the Reception

*(Copies to be given to the liquor merchant and
person in charge of the reception)*

Name of bride ——————————————— Phone —————

Address ——————————————————————————

Reception date ——————————————— Time —————

Location ——————————————————————————

Number of guests —————————————

London gin .... Brand ————————— Quantity —————
Vermouth .... Brand ————————— Quantity —————
Bonded bourbon .... Brand ————————— Quantity —————
Straight whiskey .... Brand ————————— Quantity —————
Scotch .... Brand ————————— Quantity —————
Vodka .... Brand ————————— Quantity —————
Other .... Brand ————————— Quantity —————
Other .... Brand ————————— Quantity —————
Champagne .... Brand ————————— Quantity —————
Other wines .... Brand ————————— Quantity —————
                     Brand ————————— Quantity —————.

Punch (with champagne) ————————————————————

Punch (plain) ——————————————————————

Mixers

Ginger ale ————————————————

Bitter lemon ————————————————

Tonic ————————————————

Club soda ————————————————

Cola ————————————————

Noncola ————————————————

Lemon juice ————————————————

Pineapple juice (unsweetened) —————————

Orange juice ————————————————

Tomato juice ————————————————

Alcoholic Beverages for the Reception

(Copies to be given to the liquor merchant and
person in charge of the reception)

Limes ———————————————————

Lemons ———————————————————

Oranges ———————————————————

Onions ———————————————————

Maraschino cherries ————————————

Ice ———————————————————

Equipment

   Champagne, cocktail, and tall 8-ounce glasses (no plastic glasses)

   ———————————————————

   Bottle openers —————————

   Pitchers —————————

   Knives —————————

   Large buckets for icing champagne ——————

   Small champagne buckets for bride's and parents' tables——2——————

   Ice tongs —————————

   Cocktail shakers —————————

   Ice buckets —————————

   Swizzle sticks —————————

   Cleaning cloths —————————

   Napkins —————————

Total cost of all beverages and equipment —————————————

(It's a good idea to have liquor merchant sign an agreement regarding total cost.)

Prewedding Festivities

Engagement Party

Date _____ Time _____ Location _____

_____

Host or hostess _____

Bridal Showers

Date _____ Time _____ Location _____

_____

Type of shower _____

Host or hostess _____

Date _____ Time _____ Location _____

_____

Type of shower _____

Host or hostess _____

Bride's Luncheon

Date _____ Time _____ Location _____

_____

Host or hostess (if not given by bride) _____

Bachelor Party

Date _____ Time _____ Location _____

_____

Host (if not given by groom) _____

Parties of Out-of-Town Guests

Date _____ Time _____ Location _____

_____

Host or hostess _____

Date _____ Time _____ Location _____

_____

Host or hostess _____

Rehearsal Dinner

Date _____ Time _____ Location _____

_____